Jack and the Beanstalk

A Pantomime

John Crocker

Lyrics and Music by
Eric Gilder

Samuel French–London
New York–Sydney–Toronto–Hollywood

Copyright © 1967 by John Crocker (book) and Eric Gilder (lyrics)
All Rights Reserved

JACK AND THE BEANSTALK is fully protected under the copyright laws of the British Commonwealth, including Canada, the United States of America, and all other countries of the Copyright Union. All rights, including professional and amateur stage productions, recitation, lecturing, public reading, motion picture, radio broadcasting, television and the rights of translation into foreign languages are strictly reserved.

ISBN 978-0-573-16454-5

www.samuelfrench.co.uk
www.samuelfrench.com

FOR AMATEUR PRODUCTION ENQUIRIES

UNITED KINGDOM AND WORLD
EXCLUDING NORTH AMERICA
plays@samuelfrench.co.uk
020 7255 4302/01

Each title is subject to availability from Samuel French, depending upon country of performance.

CAUTION: Professional and amateur producers are hereby warned that *JACK AND THE BEANSTALK* is subject to a licensing fee. Publication of this play does not imply availability for performance. Both amateurs and professionals considering a production are strongly advised to apply to the appropriate agent before starting rehearsals, advertising, or booking a theatre. A licensing fee must be paid whether the title is presented for charity or gain and whether or not admission is charged.

No one shall make any changes in this title for the purpose of production. No part of this book may be reproduced, stored in a retrieval system, or transmitted in any form, by any means, now known or yet to be invented, including mechanical, electronic, photocopying, recording, videotaping, or otherwise, without the prior written permission of the publisher. No one shall upload this title, or part of this title, to any social media websites.

The right of John Crocker and Eric Gilder to be identified as author(s) of this work has been asserted in accordance with Section 77 of the Copyright, Designs and Patents Act 1988.

PRODUCTION NOTE

Pantomime, as we know it today, is a form of entertainment all on its own, derived from a number of different sources - the commedia dell'arte (and all that that derived from), the ballet, the opera, the music hall and the realms of folk-lore and fairy tale. And elements of all of these are still to be found in it. This strange mixture has created a splendid topsy-turvy world where men are women, women are men, where the present is embraced within the past, where people are hit but not hurt, where authority is constantly flouted, where fun is poked at everything including pantomime itself at times, and, above all, where magic abounds and dreams invariably come true. In other words, it is - or should be - fun. Fun to do and fun to watch and the sense of enjoyment which can be conveyed by a cast is very important to the enjoyment of the audience.

Pantomime can be very simply staged if resources are limited. Basically a tab surround at the back, tab legs at the sides and a set of traverse tabs for the frontcloth scenes, together with the simplest of small cut-out pieces to suggest the various locales, (or even just placards with this information written on them), will suffice. Conversely, there is no limit to the extent to which more lavish facilities can be employed.

The directions I have given in the text adopt a middle course and are based on a permanent setting of a cyclorama skycloth at the back, a few feet in front of which is a rostrum about two feet high, running the width of the stage. About two thirds of the depth downstage is a false proscenium, immediately behind which are the lines for a set of traverse tabs. Below the false proscenium are arched entrances left and right, with possibly one foot reveals to the proscenium. A border will be necessary at some point between the false proscenium and the cyclorama to mask lighting battens and the top of the cyclorama. Lastly, there is a set of steps leading from the front of the stage into the auditorium, which I have referred to as the catwalk. I have imagined it to be set stage left, but it is unimportant whether it is left or right.

Into this permanent setting are placed various wings left and right. (I have catered for one a side set on a level with the border, but a greater depth of stage may require two a side for masking purposes.) Cut-out ground rows set on the back of the rostrum complete the full sets. On smaller stages these cut-outs seen against the cyclorama give a better impression of depth than backcloths. The frontcloth fly lines come in behind the traverse tabs. Cloths can, of course, be tumbled or rolled if flying space is limited. It is a good tip always to bring in the traverse tabs when a cloth has to be lowered, then if any hitch occurs the lights can still come up and the actors get on with the scene. Similarly, I have indicated where the traverse tabs should be closed in frontcloth scenes so that there is plenty of time for the cloth to be flown before the end of the scene. The quick flow of one scene into the next is important if a smooth running production is to be achieved.

The settings and costumes should preferably be in clear bright colours to give a story book effect. It is probably best to try to have one overall period, but which period is immaterial. Also, of course, deliberate anachronisms should be introduced into some settings and some of the comics' costumes.

Pantomime requires many props and often they will have to be home made. Instructions are given in the prop plot about any of the more awkward seeming ones. Props should also be colourfully painted and in pantomime most props should be much larger than reality. It is also wise for the property master to examine carefully the practical use to which a prop is to be put - it is very painful to be hit with a Giant's club of solid wood, one of material filled with foam plastic is far gentler.

I have not attempted to give a lighting plot as this entirely depends on the equipment available, but, generally speaking, most pantomime lighting needs to be full up, warm and bright. Pinks and ambers are probably best for this, but a circuit of blues in the cyclorama battens will help nightfall and dawn rising effects.

Follow spots are a great help for this kind of show, but not essential. But, if they are available, it is often effective in romantic numbers to fade out the stage lighting and hold the principals in the follow spots, quickly fading up on the last few bars because this often helps to increase the applause! They can also be used for the Fairy and Demon to give them greater freedom of movement than with fixed front of house or spot-bar spots.

Flash boxes, with the necessary colour and flash powders, can be obtained from the usual stage electrical suppliers and so can ultra violet equipment if it is used in Scene 5. It is very effective for the transformation if the chair, stove, the sections of the wings which are revealed in the change and other parts of the exterior set are painted with a special paint which shows up in the U.V. light, so that when they are moved by the stagehands, who should be dressed in black to make them quite invisible, they will appear to be floating about of their own volition. Similarly it adds a magical quality to the ballet and the growing of the bean-stalk if the Fairy's dress and wand, the bean costumes for the Chorus and the beanstalk are treated in the same way.

The music has been specially composed so that it is easy for the less musically accomplished to master, but it is also scored in parts for the more ambitious. If an orchestra is available well and good, but a single piano will suffice. It is an advantage, however, if there can be a drummer as well, not only because a rhythm accompaniment enhances the numbers, but also because for some reason never yet fully fathomed slapstick hits and falls are always twice as funny if they coincide with a well-timed bonk on a drum, woodblock or whatever is found to make the noise best suited to the action.

Pantomime demands a particular style of playing and production. The acting must be larger than life, but still sincere, with a good deal of sparkle and attack. Much of it must be projected directly at the audience, since one of pantomime's great advantages is that it deliberately breaks down the 'fourth wall'. The actors can literally and metaphorically shake hands with their audience who become almost another member of the cast; indeed, their active participation from time to time is essential. A word of warning, though, on this - the actors must always remain in control; for instance, if a Demon or villain encourages hissing he must make sure it is never to such an extent that he can no longer be heard. The producer should see that the story line is clearly brought out and treated with respect. There is always room for local gags and topical quips in pantomime, but they should not be overdone. Most important of all, the comedy, as any comedy, must never appear to be conscious of its own funniness.

Characterization should be very clear and definite. Bubble imagines he is highly efficient, but is really the very opposite, while Squeak is simply in search of a quiet life. Nevertheless, he frequently manages to come off better than Bubble.

King Umpty is a weak man, though still very likeable as he blusteringly tries to assert the authority and dignity he lacks.

Jack should be played as a slightly cheeky, but very romantic and adventurous young lad (but not by a young lad, for my preference).

Fairy Evergreen, for all that she is the embodiment of Good, is not above, and indeed rather enjoys, a little mischief. In brief, she should have a sense of humour. Demon Pestblight, on the other hand, has none. He is filled with a sense of his own importance, but frequently trips up over his own imcompetence. Nevertheless, he should at times still present a real menace to Jack's fortunes.

Princess Felicia also has a sense of humour and should not be played merely as a sweetly pretty little thing, rather as a not too sweetly, but certainly pretty girl, with a lively and decided mind of her own. For her, life is fun and she is determined to see that it stays that way.

Life is also fun for Dame Durden, because as she says in her first song, she has a 'happy mind'. Whatever troubles beset her they never daunt her for very long. The playing of a Dame requires a rather special balance - it should be a sincere character performance of a woman by a man, but one which never quite lets us forget it is by a man.

Simple Simon may be a little slow in the uptake, but he should have a great deal of charm and not be played as a mere numskull.

Jumping Joan is a slight enigma - a sort of wistful hockey-playing type. She is also very unselfish and outgoing with her affections. It would be best if the actress who plays her has a good sense of comedy. She will need it particularly in Scene 8, the bulk of which depends on her.

Daisy the cow is all woman - capricious, steadfast, wilful, pliant, detached and affectionate in turn. But, like all women, she is still always lovable.

The Giant is divided within himself; the two sides of his nature are, I trust, fairly obvious. It should be remembered when he actually appears that his purpose is comic and the achievement of his giant's stature should in no way detract from this.

The Pieman, I think, speaks for himself.

John Crocker

CHARACTERS

SIR BERTRAM BUBBLE	−	The Lord High Chamberlain
SIR SYDNEY SQUEAK	−	The Lord Low Chamberlain
KING UMPTY THE UMPTEENTH		
JACK DURDEN		
FAIRY EVERGREEN		
DEMON PESTBLIGHT		
DAME DURDEN	−	Jack's mother
PRINCESS FELICIA		
SIMPLE SIMON		
JUMPING JOAN		
DAISY	−	Dame Durden's cow
A PIEMAN		
GIANT BLUNDERBORE	−	A two-headed, three-legged giant

CHORUS as Villagers, Market Folk, Beans, the Elements

SYNOPSIS OF SCENES

ACT ONE

Scene 1	THE VILLAGE OF DAFFYDOWNDILLY
Scene 2	A CORRIDOR IN THE PALACE
Scene 3	THE MARKET PLACE
Scene 4	ON THE WAY HOME
Scene 5	DAME DURDEN'S COTTAGE

and Grand Transformation to −

THE GARDEN

ACT TWO

Scene 6	THE TOP OF THE BEANSTALK
Scene 7	OUTSIDE THE GIANT'S KITCHEN
Scene 8	THE GIANT'S KITCHEN
Scene 9	MEANWHILE, BACK AT HOME
Scene 10	DAME DURDEN'S GARDEN
Scene 11	BEAUTY PARLOUR
Scene 12	THE BEANFEAST AT BEANSTALK HALL

Running time, excluding interval, approximately two hours and thirty minutes

1 - 1 - 1

ACT ONE

Scene One - THE VILLAGE OF DAFFYDOWNDILLY

MUSIC 1. OVERTURE

(Full set. Cut-out representing village green at back of rostrum. There is a wing R. with a sign on it 'DAME DURDEN'S DAIRY'; there is a mop leaning against the wing. Another house wing L. U.L. a sign - 'TO THE PALACE. SEE ROUND THE ROYAL GROUNDS. 25p a BONCE'. U.C. a maypole with coloured ribbons. Steps down from rostrum.)

(CHORUS as villagers discovered dancing round maypole.)

MUSIC 2. MAYDAY

CHORUS
Mayday, Mayday is a grand and gay day
   In the very heyday of the Spring.
April showers being the sunny hours;
   There's a scent of flowers as we sing.
Spring is springing and young loves are clingin
   All the bells are ringing out to say,
'Never have there been such lovely days as these;
Birds and bees, flowering trees:
Let this lovely day go on for ever, please,
   This lovely gay Mayday'.

BUBBLE (off L.) Make way for his Majesty! Make way for his Majesty!

(MUSIC 3. BUBBLE and SQUEAK enter L. carrying two poles.)

Make way for the royal sedan chair.

CHORUS Hullo, Bubble and Squeak.

BUBBLE (stopping C.) Oh, no, no. We must have a more respectful greeting than that for the chief officers of state. I mean, what will his Majesty think?

SQUEAK But, Bubble -

BUBBLE One minute, please, Squeak. (To CHORUS.) I know that at the moment we are merely carrying the royal sedan chair -

SQUEAK But we're -

BUBBLE Squeak, I am squeaking, I mean speaking.

	(To others.) Nevertheless, I am still Sir Bertram Bubble, the Lord High Chamberlain and he is Sir Sydney Squeak, the Lord Low Chamberlain. Therefore, we must be greeted in the proper manner. Try again.
CHORUS	Hullo, Bert and Syd.
BUBBLE	No, no, no. Oh, what's the use? You'd better proceed to welcoming his Majesty.
SQUEAK	But they –
BUBBLE	Later, Squeak, we mustn't keep the King waiting. Loyal subjects, prepare to receive his most mellifluous Majesty, King Umpty the Unpteenth. (Turns in.) Your Majesty – oh.
	(CHORUS laugh.)
	We appear to have mislaid his Majesty.
SQUEAK	That's what I've been trying to tell you ever since we left the palace.
BUBBLE	Well then why didn't you? Quick, back to the palace.
	(MUSIC 4. They run off backwards D.L. KING UMPTY runs on U.L. carrying round himself a floorless sedan chair.)
KING	Bubble! Squeak! Oh, where have they got to?
CHORUS	(bowing and curtseying) Good morning, your Majesty.
KING	(stopping in C.) What? Ah, my subjects, good morn – (Tries to bow and nearly overbalances.) Oh, dear. Just a minute, good people, while I, that is, we remove ourself. (Puts down sedan, with door facing front, on his feet and gives a cry of pain, straightening up as he does so that his head shoots through the roof and he gives another cry.) Ow! My feet! My head! I mean, our feet, our head. (Opens door to step out rather grandly.) Now, my people – (Trips and falls.) Somebody take this thing away before it cripples me for life.

1 - 1 - 3

(Two of CHORUS take sedan off L. and return.)

What were you saying, my dear populace?

CHORUS (bowing and curtseying) Good morning, your Majesty.

KING Ah, yes indeed. Good morning.

(MUSIC 5. KING starts to bow as BUBBLE and SQUEAK run on backwards with the poles, BUBBLE leading.)

BUBBLE We must have missed him.

(BUBBLE bumps into KING's behind and knocks him over. CHORUS laugh.)

KING Aah!

BUBBLE So sorry. Can't stop. Looking for the King.

(BUBBLE and SQUEAK run off R.)

KING (rising) I fail to see anything humorous in the situation. And I was just in the middle of saying something when it happened.

CHORUS Good morning.

KING Of course. Well, good m— (Is about to bow, but stops and looks off L.) Ah, all clear. Good morning. (Bows.)

(MUSIC 6. BUBBLE and SQUEAK enter R., BUBBLE still leading backwards.)

BUBBLE Come on. (Bumps into KING and knocks him down again.)

KING Aah!

BUBBLE Beg pardon. Can't stop. Must find his Majesty.

(BUBBLE and SQUEAK run off.)

KING These hit and run pedestrians are getting a menace. Now, I'm here to make a most important announcement. The wicked Giant Blunderbore threatens to ravage our land again unless we pay him double his usual dues. Therefore all outstanding rent must be paid by noon today, plus twice the usual Giant tax.

CHORUS	Twice the usual tax! Oh, it's not fair! By noon! We shall be ruined! Where's the money to come from, etc.
KING	Ah, my people, my heart bleeds for you. But how else can we deal with the Giant?
	(Enter JACK DURDEN U.R.)
JACK	We can fight him.
KING	I beg your pardon?
CHORUS	It's Jack! Hullo, Jack.
	<u>MUSIC 7.</u>
KING	Jack? Jack who?
JACK	(coming D.S.) Jack Durden. You're the King, aren't you?
KING	I am, I mean, we am, I mean - yes. What's all this foolish talk of fighting the Giant?
JACK	It's not nearly so foolish as paying to keep him quiet. The more we pay the more he wants. So why not let's try fighting him?
1st CHORUS	Because we'd all be killed.
JACK	We wouldn't. I bet you we'd kill him.
KING	Kill the Giant! Oh no, that might really upset him. Really, I don't know where you get such dangerous notions from, Master Durden, but - Ah, wait a minute, Durden. You must be the son of that dairy woman, Dame Durden.
JACK	That's right.
KING	Then no wonder you've thought up this harebrained scheme - so your mother won't have to pay her debts. She owes more rent and taxes than anybody in the kingdom.
JACK	I'm not surprised. She's owed more than anybody. For instance, the palace milk bill hasn't been paid for ten years.
KING	Yes, well, er - (Looks at watch.) I see, it's Friday. Time for me to sign on at the

	Labour Exchange. We must leave you now, my people. Good morning. (Bows.)
	(MUSIC 8. Enter BUBBLE and SQUEAK backwards L., BUBBLE leading.)
BUBBLE	We're bound to run into him soon. (Bumps into KING and knocks him down.)
KING	Aah!
BUBBLE	Sorry. Can't stop. Still looking for the King.
	(BUBBLE and SQUEAK run off R. KING rises.)
KING	Oh no! This is too bad. I'll summons them for careless running. Come back here! Come back! (He runs off R.)
JACK	I was afraid he wouldn't listen, but I'm sure I'm right all the same. But why didn't any of you back me up? Don't you want adventures?
CHORUS	Not those kind of adventures.
JACK	Well, I do. I want to go out into the world and do all the exciting things there are to do. I want to live.

MUSIC 9. I WANT TO LIVE

I want to dance,
   I want to sing, sing, sing,
I want to laugh
   Because it's Spring, Spring, Spring.
With all the wild excitement that the future has to
                                 give,
I want to live, I want to live, I want to live.
The world's a book;
   I like the trend of it;
I want to look
   Right to the end of it.
I want to travel oceans and I won't go in a sieve –
I want to live, I want to live, I want to live.
The world has seven wonders, and
   There's seven million more:
I really want to understand
   What life's worth living for.
Get out the map!

The die is cast for me.
I feel the sap
   Is rising fast in me.
I'm young and I am healthy and the world has much
      to give –
I want to live, I want to live, I want to live.

(JACK and CHORUS go off. BLACKOUT. WHITE SPOT on FAIRY EVERGREEN as she enters R. MUSIC 10.)

FAIRY   Greetings, good mortals, I am here
Jack Durden's destinies to steer
Toward renown and fortunes high,
Since guardian of the youth am I.
My name is Fairy Evergreen –
Where'er things grow is my demesne,
And all my verdant realms do thrive
Provided I 'gainst evil strive.
But there's the rub – 'twould seem of late
That evil's in a parlous state,
For Demon Pestblight, my pledg'd foe,
Now ne'er his power tries to show.
But stay! I'm wrong, for here he comes.
Beware, the smoke and crash of drums.

(MUSIC 11. FAIRY puts hands over her ears. DRUM CRASH and GREEN FLASH L. GREEN SPOT on DEMON PESTBLIGHT as he enters L.)

Why must thy entry cause such noise?

DEMON   Thy pardon if it spoils thy poise,
But I'm not on thy comfort bent,
I've come to show my pow'r's not spent.

FAIRY   What kept thee then so long away?

DEMON   Why, nothing.

FAIRY   Nothing?

DEMON   Aye.

FAIRY   Oh, nay!

I think to tell ye are afraid.

DEMON   Since thou must know, I had mislaid
A book on which my skill relied –

1 - 1 - 7

'The Necromancer's Black Arts Guide'.

(FAIRY starts to laugh.)

Pray, what does cause thy mirthful zest?

FAIRY   The large result of my small jest,
Which I had quite forgot till now.
'Twas I mislaid thy book, not thou.
I hid it but for passing sport,
Not thinking 'twould thy pow'r so thwart.

DEMON   Thou wilt regret thy hum'rous slight,
For I shall now exert my might
Till I do reign the whole world o'er!
And that I may this end ensure
Thy cherish'd ward I'll make my prey
And haste his fortunes to betray!

(DEMON goes off L.)

FAIRY   He is himself once more, I see,
Which, truth to tell, much pleases me;
For, 'twixt ourselves, I find our strife
The spice of my immortal life!

(FAIRY goes off R. SPOT OUT and LIGHTS UP. Clatter and banging heard off L.)

DAME   (off L.)   Stop, you silly thing, stop!

(MUSIC 12. DAME DURDEN enters L. buffeted on by a small motorised hand-drawn milk-float, on top of which is a sign 'DURDEN'S DAIRY' and 'DRINKA PINTA MILKA (STOUTA) DAY'.)

Oops, nark it, now, nark it! Look out!

(It knocks her flat on her face.)

Ow!   (Rises.)   You're supposed to be a milk float, not a milk buffet.   (Sees audience.)
Oh, people - how lovely, now I shan't have to talk to myself.   (Curtseying.)   How do you do?
I'm Dame Durden. How are you, all right?
(Listens for reaction.)   Dear me, you can't be as bad as all that. I'll try again. How are you, all right?   (Gets them to answer 'yes'.)
Ah, that's better. Ooh, look - there's a party here have brought their musical instruments with

them. Isn't that nice? Are you in charge, dear? What's your name?

(CONDUCTOR gives name. DAME repeats it.)

Well, I do hope you can all stay, because I'm sure you'll come in useful later. (To audience.) I've had a terrible morning trying to do me milk round. Me milk float wouldn't stop. And now I'm all shaken to bits. Well, I started out to deliver three dozen pints of milk and here I am back again with three dozen pounds of butter. And what it's done to me stays, I don't know. One moment they were down round me ankles tripping me up and the next up round me neck strangling me. In fact, they weren't so much stays as moves. I've lost track of them altogether now. (Lifts skirt to find them.) No, it's all right, they've returned to base - if you see what I mean. Of course, my son Jack's supposed to do the milk round, but he's always out looking for adventures. Still he's a great comfort to a poor widow like me. I used to have a daughter too, but she was stolen away as a tiny mite. (Begins to cry.) Ah, poor little scrap.

(CHORUS enter L. and R.)

CHORUS   What's the matter, Mrs Durden? Don't cry.

2nd CHORUS   You're supposed to be happy today. It's Mayday.

DAME   So it is. (Patting her hair.) Have you chosen the May Queen yet?

3rd CHORUS   No, but -

DAME   Splendid, then now's your chance.

4th CHORUS   Well, Simple Simon's going to be the judge this year.

DAME   Simple Simon? My cowman who looks after my cow, Daisy? But he's so shy with girls. Daisy's the only female he can look in the face. He'll probably choose her. You'd much better settle for me.

5th CHORUS   But all the candidates have to be under twenty-one.

DAME	Well, I'm not far off if you count quickly. Still, youth must have its fling, I suppose, and I certainly flung mine. Ah, I remember May Day when I was young. Year after year my mother had to wake me early in the morning. It never did a bit of good though - I was always the early worm that got the bird.

<u>MUSIC 13.</u> ALSO RAN   Words and Music by
John Crocker

	I've always been an also ran, Sometimes a runner-up, Upon my beauty there's a ban, It's never won a cup. Except when I was very young Upon a bearskin rug; And then it was the rug that won And not my ugly mug.
CHORUS	And then it was the rug that won And not her ugly mug.
DAME	In eighteen ninety-nine, my dears, Or was it ninety-eight? They made me be, despite my fears, Show-jumping candidate. My turn-out seem'd to me a mess It wasn't quite my size, But 'cos they thought I was the horse I nearly won first prize.
CHORUS	But 'cos they thought she was the horse She nearly won first prize.
DAME	At ev'rything I have a go, But even lose at whist, For years I've stood 'neath mistletoe, But never yet been kiss'd. Yet I don't really care, you see, Though fate may be unkind, I know the secret of this life -
CHORUS	You know the secret of this life?
DAME	I know the secret of this life, I have a happy mind.

1 - 1 - 10

	(She starts to go off R., pulling the milkfloat, but it goes into reverse and pulls her protesting off L. MUSIC 14. Enter PRINCESS FELICIA R.)
FELICIA	Hullo.
	(CHORUS turn; boys kneel and girls curtsey.)
CHORUS	Your Highness.
FELICIA	Oh no, do get up, please.
	(CHORUS rise.)
	I spend half my life at court seeing only the tops of people's heads and it gets very boring. Now, I've some news for my father. Have any of you seen him?
6th CHORUS	Yes, he's running around looking for Bubble and Squeak.
FELICIA	Then where are Bubble and Squeak?
1st CHORUS	Running around looking for him.
	(MUSIC 15. ENTRANCE MUSIC. BUBBLE and SQUEAK run on R., with the poles.)
BUBBLE	Do stop dawdling, Squeak.
SQUEAK	(very breathless) But I'm - I'm -
FELICIA	Hey, Bubble, Squeak -
BUBBLE	Squeak, her Highness.
	(They double-mark time L., and bow as they do so.)
	Good morning, your Highness.
	(They start running again and BUBBLE bumps into wing L.)
	Ooh! Squeak, please look where I'm going.
	(They trot off L.)
FELICIA	Ah well, perhaps Father will pay us a flying visit soon.
	(MUSIC 16. ENTRANCE MUSIC. KING runs on R.)

1 - 1 - 11

	Father!
KING	(wheeling round and stopping just past her, double-marking time) Sorry, my dear, can't stop. (Starts running again, but to R.) Oh no, wrong way. (He wheels round and runs off L.)
FELICIA	(laughing) Hopeless. I'll have to tell him later. You see, apparently the Giant is sending his daughter to collect the money today.
CHORUS	His daughter?
2nd CHORUS	I didn't know he had a daughter.
FELICIA	Nor did I. I hope she won't have the same appetite as her father - so awkward if she gobbles up the reception committee. Anyway, at least we shan't have the Giant himself fee-fo-fumming around.
3rd CHORUS	You don't seem very worried about her.
FELICIA	Me? I'm hardly ever worried about anything. If you worry you can't enjoy yourself, and -

MUSIC 17. ENJOYING MYSELF

I like enjoying myself
And having a lot of fun.
I like to laugh and dance and sing
Stand on my head and ev'rything.
I'm not a stick in the mud
Who goes around feeling blue -
I just enjoy just enjoying myself,
Don't you?

Some old lazybones
Sit around all day;
Some old sleepyheads
Dream their lives away;
I'm up with the lark,
(There's one goes up at ten!)
I leap out of bed
And life's begun again.

(She goes off L. Loud crash off R.)

| SIMON | (off R.)   Ow! |

1 - 1 - 12

4th CHORUS	What's that?
	(Louder crash off R.)
SIMON	(off R.) Ow!
CHORUS	It's Simple Simon.
	(MUSIC 18. Enter SIMPLE SIMON U.R. with a blindfold round his eyes.)
	Hullo, Simple Simon.
SIMON	Hullo. (Crashes into maypole.) Ow! Sorry.
5th CHORUS	That's the maypole, Simon.
SIMON	Is it? (Pulls down blindfold.) Oh yes. (Moves across maypole, sees CHORUS GIRLS.) Gosh, girls. (Pulls blindfold up, turns and crashes into L. side of maypole.) Ow! Sorry. (Touches maypole.) Um, haven't we met before?
6th CHORUS	It's the maypole again.
SIMON	Oh. It's this blindfold, you know. It makes it difficult to see where you're going.
1st CHORUS	Then don't wear it.
SIMON	Oh, I must. It's part of my May Queen choosing equipment. You see, I get a bit shy with girls, but if I wear this I'm all right.
2nd CHORUS	But how are you going to choose one of us if you can't see us?
SIMON	Ah, that's where the other part of my May Queen choosing equipment comes in.
3rd CHORUS	What's that?
SIMON	(taking out steel knitting needle) This pin.
	(CHORUS GIRLS shriek and run U.S.)
	No, don't make a noise yet. Wait until you're chosen. Right, stand by.
	(MUSIC 19. BUBBLE and SQUEAK run on L. with poles.)
SQUEAK	(gasping) I - I -

1 - 1 - 13

SIMON	(plunging pin into SQUEAK's behind.) You're the winner.
SQUEAK	Waah!
BUBBLE	Save your breath for running, Squeak.
	(MUSIC 20. They go off R. KING runs on L.)
SIMON	And you're the runner up. (Plunges pin into KING's behind.)
KING	Waah! Help! I've been assassinated! (He runs off R.)
4th CHORUS	I think we'd better go. Come on!
	(They run off L. and R. SIMON removes blindfold.)
SIMON	There. Oh, they've gone. Well, they might have let me see which one I chose. (Sees audience.) Ooh. Oh dear, girls. I - er - that is, I - well - I - I'm shy, you know, and - well, goodbye. (Turns and runs U.S., crashes into maypole and rises, rubbing forehead.) Now I'm painfully shy. I really must do something about it. Ah, I've got an idea. I'll get all of you to help me. Every time I feel nervous I shall say, 'Help, please!" and all of you must shout back, 'Steady, Simon!' and then I shall be all right. Let's try it. Help, please! (Waits for reaction.) Oh no, you'll have to do better than that. I get a bit deaf when I'm nervous. I'll try again. Help, please! (Waits for reaction.) Better, I heard it very well in this ear, but not so well in this one. I'll try just once more. Help, please! (Waits for reaction.) Ah, that's it. Now I -
	(A thump is heard off L.)
	Was that an echo?
	(Another thump.)
	I don't think it can have been.
	(Another thump.)
	(Moving to look off L.) I wonder what it is?
	(MUSIC 21. Enter JUMPING JOAN L., singing

1 - 1 - 14

                  and proceeding in a series of leaps. She jumps right round SIMON, who stands rooted to the spot, watching her progress round him by turning his head. She ends up on his L.)

JOAN	Here am I, Little Jumping Joan. When nobody's with me I'm always alone, All alone, all alone, always alone. All alone, all alone, always alone.
SIMON	Oh.
JOAN	(jumping a little closer)　Oh, what?
SIMON	(jumping away)　You're a girl.
JOAN	(jumping in)　I know.
SIMON	(tries to jump away, but finds himself up against Dairy)　Well - oh dear - I - er - I -　Ah! (Moves down to audience.)　Help, please!
AUDIENCE	Steady, Simon!
SIMON	Oh, very good, and it works a treat. I feel a new man.　(Turning back.)　Now then, Miss - oh I say, you're rather - er - rather - well, you are, aren't you?
JOAN	And so are you.
SIMON	Oh no, I'm not pretty. Ooh, there - I've said it. I'm getting very bold for me.
JOAN	And who is me?
SIMON	Simple Simon. Who are you?
JOAN	I'm not quite sure, really. You see my father's not my real father. He said he just found me, but I think he stole me away. He calls me Jumping Joan. That's because I jump, you know.
SIMON	Why?
JOAN	I have to where I live, the furniture's so high. Why, I even have to jump just to get on the carpet. You see, the man who calls himself my father is very big.
SIMON	What else does he call himself, besides your father?

1 - 1 - 15

JOAN	If I tell you, will you promise not to run away?
SIMON	Of course, why should I run away?
JOAN	Because he's the Giant.
SIMON	The Giant? Oh, really? Well, of course, Giants are big - the Giant! (Runs off R.)
JOAN	Simon!
SIMON	(peering on R.) Y-y-yes?
JOAN	You promised.
SIMON	I know, but - (Gulps.) Well, are you sure you haven't picked up any gianty habits - like eating people?
JOAN	Oh no, certainly not.
SIMON	(coming onstage) I'm so glad. I'd much rather be your boy friend than your dinner.
JOAN	My boy friend? What a nice thought. I haven't any friends, you know. That's why I always sing -
	<u>MUSIC 22.</u> JUMPING JOAN Additional Words and Music by John Crocker
	Here am I, Little Jumping Joan. When nobody's with me I'm always alone, All alone, all alone, always alone, All alone, all alone, always alone.
SIMON	I'm here now, Silly Simple Si. And when I am with you I don't feel so shy. Not so shy.
JOAN	Nor do I.
BOTH	We see eye to eye.
JOAN	I to you.
SIMON	You to I.
BOTH	We're eye to eye.
JOAN	I'm so glad That I have met you.

	We weren't introduc'd.
SIMON	Well then, how do you do?
JOAN	How do you do?
SIMON	How do you do?
BOTH	How do you do? How do you do? How do you do? How do you do?
	You and me, Simple Si and Joan, When we are together we'll ne'er be alone. Never more, never more, never more alone. Never more, never more, never alone.
	(There is a scream off L. and DAME DURDEN runs on.)
DAME	Ah! Help! Help! I've just seen the Giant. (She runs off into dairy.)
SIMON and JOAN	The Giant!
	MUSIC 23.
GIANT	(off L.) Fee-fi-fo-fum!
	(Screams from CHORUS off L.)
JOAN	Don't worry, Simon, I'll go and stop him before he does any damage. (Running off L.) Father! Father!
	(A roar from the GIANT and more screams from CHORUS as they run on L.)
CHORUS	Run! Run! The Giant! (Exeunt R.)
SIMON	Oh dear. (To audience.) H-help, please!
AUDIENCE	Steady, Simon.
SIMON	That's better. I'm not nervous now.
	(BUBBLE and SQUEAK run on with poles R., SQUEAK practically on his knees.)
BUBBLE	No lagging, Squeak, I think I heard the King's voice.
	(They run off L.)

SIMON	No, I'm not nervous. I'm not nervous!
	(Another roar from the GIANT. BUBBLE and SQUEAK return running helter-skelter from L.)
BUBBLE	Anybody can make a mistake.
	(They rush off R.)
GIANT	(off L.) Fee-fi-fo-fum! I smell the blood of an Englishman.
	(KING bolts on L.)
KING	It's a lie! I'm not English! I'm not! (KING tears off R.)
SIMON	I'm still not nervous! I'm still not nervous!
GIANT	(off L.) Be he alive or be he dead, I'll grind his bones to make my bread!
SIMON	I am nervous!
	(He turns and runs off R. BLACKOUT. WHITE FLASH. WHITE SPOT on FAIRY as she enters R.)
FAIRY	Avaunt, thou evil Giant, away! I do command! Begone, I say!
	(To audience.)
	That nearly all my hopes did dash. Young Jack hastes here like lightning flash Eager to meet the Giant in fight; But 'tis too soon for trials of might, And I did rather have in mind A meeting of another kind Where Jack his thoughts t'ward love might steer, For see - I've brought the Princess here.
	(FAIRY goes off R. LIGHTS UP. Enter FELICIA L. JACK runs on R.)
JACK	Where is this Giant? (Sees FELICIA.) Oh. Do you want rescuing?
FELICIA	Yes, please - but what from?
JACK	The Giant, of course.
FELICIA	I'm afraid you're too late, then. He's gone away again. But thank you all the same, er - ?

1 - 1 - 18

JACK	Jack Durden.
FELICIA	Oh - Father spoke about you, but I think he's wrong. You're very nice.
JACK	Thank you. I think you're very nice, too. What's your father got against me, though? Who is he, anyway?
FELICIA	Umpty.
JACK	I beg your pardon?
FELICIA	Umpty. That's his name. Umpty the Umpteenth.
JACK	Then you're the Princess. Well - I've never met a princess before.
FELICIA	Don't let it worry you. I'm only a girl, really.
JACK	And I'm only a boy.
FELICIA	Then we should go very well together.

MUSIC 24. SO SHOULD WE

BOTH
As certain things go well together,
So should we,
Like ham and eggs and hell for leather,
So should we.
So many pairs of things there are,
I think we should discuss
How we can find a formula
To fit the two of us.
There's cream and strawberries, bread and butter,
Cakes and ale;
But screw our courage to the utter,
We'll not fail!
The thought that two and two make four
Applies to you and me;
So if all the other things can make a happy pair of it,
So can we!

(They go off R. GREEN FLASH L. MUSIC 25. Enter DEMON L.)

DEMON
A plague upon the female sex,
This Princess all my plans will vex.
Doubtless this is some fairy game
To help Jack win renown and fame.

Then I his doom must expedite
And on such hopes thus cast a blight.
For this the King shall be my tool,
I'll draw him hence, the poor old fool.
(Makes mesmeric drawing movements with hands to R.)
Come to my call, I summon thee!

(MUSIC 26. KING runs on backwards L.)

Where is he then?

(KING bumps into DEMON.)

KING   Oops, pardon me.

DEMON   (turns)   Thou dolt! Thou clod! Stay, art the King?

KING   I am, but it's a most strange thing,
I just got here with such a jerk.

DEMON   (aside)   My magic now doth backwards work.
(Bows.)   Thy pardon for my harsh words, sire,
To slight thee is my last desire.

KING   We do forgive thee.

DEMON   Ah, how kind,
Such monarchs one does rarely find.
I've long admir'd thee from afrar.

KING   Oh, really?

DEMON   Aye, but some there are
Do not respect thee as they should,
Do mock thy laws and doubt their good.

KING   What! Who dares question aught I say?

DEMON   That Durden lad ye met today.
And now, behind thy back, he's plann'd
To try and win thy daughter's hand.

KING   My daughter?

DEMON   Yes.

KING   I am quite vex'd.

Presumptuous youth! Whatever next?
Something or other must be done.

But what?

DEMON
Ah, such a sense of fun!
For one who is as wise as you
To feign he knows not what to do.

KING
Well, yes, of course, I do know, but
My memory has just gone phut.
Prithee remind me of the sort
Of thought you thought I ought've thought.

DEMON
Why, you did think that it were wise
To humble him in others' eyes;
And since Dame Durden, as all know,
Much rent and tax to thee doth owe,
Eviction struck you as the way.

KING
I really thought all that you say?

DEMON
Aye.

KING
Clever me! How simply grand!
I'll straightway put my plan in hand
As soon as I can chance to spy
My Chamberlains both Low and High.

(MUSIC 27. Enter BUBBLE and SQUEAK at R. side of auditorium with poles to go across a transverse aisle. HOUSELIGHTS UP.)

DEMON
Well, there they go.

KING
(running to catwalk)   Hey, you two, stop!

BUBBLE
We can't.

SQUEAK
Then I shall soon go pop.

(They go out at L. side of auditorium. KING runs over catwalk to follow them.)

KING
Oh, blow! They've gone.

DEMON
They will be back.

(MUSIC 27A. BUBBLE and SQUEAK re-enter at L. side of auditorium and return along transverse aisle.)

BUBBLE
Dear me, a ladies' cul-de-sac.

(They go out R. of auditorium.)

1 - 1 - 21

KING   I'll catch them now. Goodbye and thanks.

       (KING goes out at R. side of auditorium. HOUSELIGHTS OUT. DEMON bows, then laughs, rubbing his hands.)

DEMON   I think that's settled young Jack's pranks!
       So I'll await in yonder oak
       The outcome of my master stroke.
       (Goes off L.)

DAME   (off R.) Daisy! Daisy! Where are you, Daisy?

DAISY   (off L.) Moo!

       (MUSIC 28. DAISY the Cow skips playfully on U.L., and stops U.C., puts her head on one side and scratches it with her L. rear leg. She registers audience and comes D.C., waves a foreleg, then executes two magnificent curtseys, first to R. side with the L. legs, then to L. with the R. legs. Unfortunately second curtsey is so elaborate she cannot get up again.)

       Moo!

DAME   (off R.) Daisy! Daisy! (Enters R. from Dairy.) Ah, there she is, the dear old thing. Isn't she lovely? Have you been saying how do you do, Daisy?

       (DAISY nods.)

       Oh, you are a clever girl. Well, up you get now then.

DAISY   (trying to indicate that she cannot) Moo!

DAME   What? Oh, I see, you can't.

       (DAISY shakes her head.)

       Never mind, I'll help you. (Grasps her rear half.) Come on, ups-a-daisy, Daisy.
       (She gets rear half upright.) That's right.
       (Grasps the front half.) Now this bit, dear.

       (She gets front half up and rear half subsides.)

       There we are. (Sees rear half down.)
       Daisy, you're not trying. And you're being very

1 - 1 - 22

    trying not trying. (Gets under DAISY's tummy and DAISY is upright for a moment.) There, you see - all it needs is a little concentration.

    (DAISY collapses with DAME underneath her, on her stomach facing front.)

    Anyone here got a car-jack? Simon! Simon! Come and get me out of here.

SIMON   (poking head on from Dairy) Did you call me, Mrs Durden?

DAME   Yes.

SIMON   Well, I'm not coming. (Disappears.)

DAME   What do you mean? Come back!

SIMON   (popping head on again) No. I don't want the Giant to eat me up.

DAME   But the Giant went away ages ago.

SIMON   Well, I still feel nervous. (To audience.) Help, please!

AUDIENCE   Steady, Simon!

SIMON   Ah, that's all right. (Strides onstage.) Now then. I say - did you know you've got Daisy on top of you?

DAME   Of course I did. That's why I called you, to get her off me. I can't stay here all day.

SIMON   Why, are you doing anything special?

DAME   Oh, just shift Daisy.

SIMON   All right. (Tugging DAISY up.) Come on, Daisy, up you come, up, up, up.

    (DAME crawls from under her as DAISY rises until the rear half is standing up straight and close to the front half.)

    There - oh, she's turned into a camel.

DAME   Very versatile animal. Spread out a bit, dear.

    (DAISY's rear half moves to its proper position.)

    After that nasty experience I think you deserve a

1 - 1 - 23

bit of cattle cake.

(DAISY agrees wholeheartedly and runs toward Dairy.)

But only a piece, mind.

DAISY   Moo.

DAME   Two? Oh, very well.

(DAISY goes off R. Enter JACK L.)

JACK   Mother, the King's on his way to evict us!

DAME and SIMON   To evict us!

(Enter KING L.)

KING   To evict you! Unless you pay all your debts immediately.

DAME   Immediately! But -

KING   Too late. You leave me no alternative but to evict you. General Bubble!

(Enter BUBBLE L., as a General. He salutes smartly.)

BUBBLE   Sir?

KING   Evict these people.

BUBBLE   (saluting even more smartly) Very good, sir. (About-turns so enthusiastically that he comes face to face with KING again.) Oh. (Unwinds himself.) Royal Army!

(Enter SQUEAK L. as a Private, carrying a rifle.)

SQUEAK   Yes?

BUBBLE   Evict these people.

(SQUEAK looks at others and counts them, then produces a little white flag.)

SQUEAK   The army's outnumbered. It surrenders.

OTHERS   Hurray!

KING   The army never surrenders. General Bubble, get the battle started. I shall return when you

                                                           1 - 1 - 24

                        are victorious.

BUBBLE   Yes, sir.   (Salutes too smartly and hits
                        himself.)   Ow!

                        (KING goes off R.)

                        Private Squeak, put away that white flag. They
                        won't show any resistance.

SQUEAK   (putting flag away)   Promise?

DAME   Oh yes, we shall. We shall fight.

SIMON   F-fight?

DAME   Yes, fight! We shall fight them on the doorstep,
                        in the parlour, on the stairs, in the bathroom!

SIMON   Why in the bathroom?

DAME   Well, we want this to be a clean fight.

BUBBLE   Oh yes, and to make sure it is I'll have an arms
                        inspection.   (To SQUEAK.)   Show me your
                        arms.

                        (SQUEAK holds out his arms.)

                        No, no, I am referring to lethal weapons.

SQUEAK   Oh.   (Shows BUBBLE his rifle.)

JACK   What are we going to use?

SIMON   How about this?   (Takes mop resting against
                        Dairy.)

JACK   What can we use that for?

SIMON   Mopping up operations, of course.

BUBBLE   (returning rifle)   Lovely. Now prepare to
                        attack!

                        (SQUEAK raises rifle aggressively, but unfortunate-
                        ly holding it butt first and biffing BUBBLE with it.)

                        Ow!

DAME   Ah, first blood to us! Prepare to defend!

                        (SIMON raises mop aggressively, unfortunately
                        jabbing DAME in behind with the handle.)

1 - 1 - 25

	Ow!
BUBBLE	Ah, a successful attack in the rear! Army, charge!
SQUEAK	Charge who?
BUBBLE	The enemy.
SQUEAK	How much?
BUBBLE	We don't charge them anything.
SQUEAK	Oh, it's a free fight, is it?
BUBBLE	Stop mucking about. Bring up the artillery!
	(Exit SQUEAK L.)
JACK, DAME and SIMON	The artillery!
JACK	Mother, we must do something.
DAME	Yes, dear, we will.
JACK and SIMON	What?
DAME	Run!
	(They run off R. SQUEAK wheels on large prop cannon from L.)
BUBBLE	I'll sight it. (Looks along barrel.) Up a bit.
	(SQUEAK tilts barrel right up and hits BUBBLE in face.)
	Ouch! Down a bit.
	(SQUEAK tilts it right down to point at ground.)
	No, no, level it off.
	(SQUEAK swivels barrel so it completes a quarter circle and points to L.)
	That's right. Fire!
SQUEAK	Where? I'll get some water.
BUBBLE	Fire the cannon!
SQUEAK	Oh. Are you sure this is right?

		1 - 1 - 26

BUBBLE: Of course. Oh. (Moves barrel round to point R.) How can you be so careless, Squeak? Now, fire!

(SQUEAK pulls lever at back of cannon and he and BUBBLE put their hands over their ears. Nothing happens. JACK, DAME and SIMON peer on R.)

Very slow fuse. (Looks into front of barrel.)

SQUEAK: I've just remembered something. (Exit L.)

BUBBLE: What?

SQUEAK: (staggering on with large prop cannon ball) This. (Loads it into front of cannon.)

BUBBLE: How remiss of you, Squeak. Now, no more mistakes, please. Fire!

(JACK, DAME and SIMON hurriedly disappear. SQUEAK pulls lever. The cannon ball is pushed out, but only just. JACK and SIMON run on R.)

JACK and SIMON: Missed! (They pick up cannon ball and hold it high.)

BUBBLE: Quick, get some more ammunition and fire again.

SQUEAK: We haven't any.

BUBBLE: I don't care, get some.

SQUEAK: Oh, all right. (Crosses to JACK and SIMON.) Can we have our ball back, please?

JACK and SIMON: Certainly! (They crash it down on SQUEAK's head and he sinks to the floor.)

BUBBLE: I say, that's not cricket.

SIMON: No, football. (Kicks ball off L., then hops around holding foot in pain.)

DAME: (off R.) Cavalry! Charge!

(She gallops on, mounted on DAISY, holding the mop like a lance, with which she buffets BUBBLE in the face and he falls prostrate on top of SQUEAK. DAME dismounts and DAISY puts a foot on BUBBLE. MUSIC 29.)

DAME, JACK and SIMON	Victory!
	(Enter KING and FELICIA L. and CHORUS L. and R.)
KING	Splendid! You see, my dear, one can always rely on Bubble and Squeak. Eh? Bubble and Squeak, what has happened?
BUBBLE and SQUEAK	(sitting up, rubbing their heads) We lost.
KING	Then you ought to be ashamed of yourselves. Now I suppose I'll have to give them time to pay.
ALL	Hurray!
KING	But only until next market day. As for the rest of you, it's nearly noon and the Giant's daughter -
	(JOAN jumps on R. and pulls KING's sleeve.)
JOAN	I say.
KING	Quiet, girl, I'm busy. The Giant's daughter will be here soon -
JOAN	(tugging his sleeve again) As a matter of fact -
KING	This is too bad. Bubble, Squeak, don't just sit there - remove this wretched, interfering girl.
BUBBLE and SQUEAK	(rising) Yes, your Majesty. (Hustling JOAN off.) Come along, madam.
KING	As I was saying about the Giant's daughter -
SIMON	But she is the Giant's daughter.
KING	What? Bubble, Squeak, what are you thinking of? Release her Giantess-ship immediately. Dear lady, pray accept my apologies. I'm afraid we haven't quite collected the money yet, but -
JOAN	It doesn't matter, that's what I've come to tell you. I've persuaded Father not to double the levy after all.
ALL	Hurray!
KING	Splendid news! This calls for a celebration. As it's May Day, let's celebrate with a holiday.

ALL　　　　　　　Yes!

(MUSIC 30. MAYDAY - Reprise 2

BLACKOUT

Close traverse tabs. Fly in Scene 2 frontcloth
as soon as ready.)

ACT ONE

Scene Two - A CORRIDOR IN THE PALACE

(MUSIC 31. GREEN FLASH L. and GREEN SPOT on to DEMON as he enters L. in front of tabs.)

DEMON
A murrain on these mortal folk!
They've jigger'd up my master stroke,
And let Jack 'scape my evil guile;
But he shall only 'scape a while.
Meantime, lest she a menace prove,
Methinks this Princess I'll remove.
And, since he'll relish such a task,
I'll Blunderbore the Giant ask
To carry off the damsel fair
And hide her safe within his lair.
I'll go to him without delay
And seal her fate for market day!

(Exit DEMON L. LIGHTS UP and tabs open to reveal a Palace Corridor frontcloth, if used. MUSIC 32. BUBBLE hobbles on R. with his L. arm in a sling, his R. leg in a footsling and supporting himself on a crutch under his right arm.)

BUBBLE
I don't think I'll go on any more military manoeuvres. (Calling to R.) Squeak! Squeak! Hurry up with that first aid.

SQUEAK
(off R.) Coming.

(He staggers on R. under the weight of a large box marked with a red cross and on U.S. side the words 'SECOND AID'. He has a huge bandage round his head. He trips over BUBBLE's crutch and topples him down.)

BUBBLE
Do be careful. Help me up.

SQUEAK
Yes, all right. (Plonks box down on BUBBLE's L. foot.)

BUBBLE
Aah! That was my good foot.

SQUEAK
Oh, beg pardon. (Lifts box and plonks it on BUBBLE's R. foot.)

BUBBLE
Waah! Sydney Squeak, take that thing off my feet!

1 - 2 - 30

SQUEAK	(moving box to between them) Well, I was only trying to help. Here. Why's your arm in a sling? What's happened to it?
BUBBLE	Nothing, but it was feeling tired. Now, let's have some first aid. (Turns box to show words.) Well, where's the First Aid, then?
SQUEAK	(taking a bottle from pocket) Here.
BUBBLE	How can that be first aid?
SQUEAK	Well, it aids you when you're firsty.
BUBBLE	Ah, you mean it's lemonade.
SQUEAK	No, first aid. (Turns bottle round to show it is labelled 'WHISKY' in large letters.)
BUBBLE	Perhaps you're right. (Takes bottle and has a swig.) Ah, deliciously medicinal. Let's have a look at the second aid then.
	(BUBBLE leans forward and is hit in the face by the lid of the box as SQUEAK lifts it.)
	Ow!
SQUEAK	Sorry. Now what do you fancy? (Takes out some forceps.) How about some forceps?
BUBBLE	No, I'm not really hungry. I don't think I could manage one sep let alone four. I think we ought to just clean our wounds.
SQUEAK	Right, here's some iodine. (Replaces forceps and takes out a bottle.)
BUBBLE	Oh dear, that stings, doesn't it? You'd better give me a local anaesthetic first.
SQUEAK	Very well. (Replaces bottle and takes out huge hypodermic syringe.)
BUBBLE	The thought of pain makes me quite feverish, you know.
SQUEAK	Feverish? I'd better take your temperature.
	(Takes a large thermometer from box and pops it into BUBBLE's mouth. BUBBLE gives a protesting gurgle.)

	No, no don't talk. Just come here so I can apply the anaesthetic.
	(BUBBLE sidles towards SQUEAK with face averted and a hand over his eyes and backs onto the hypodermic.)
BUBBLE	Aah! (Leaps away, turning U. S. to drop the thermometer from his mouth out of sight, then wheels round.) Ooh! I've swallowed the thermometer.
SQUEAK	Well, that was silly. Now how am I going to read it?
BUBBLE	Never mind that. Get it out.
SQUEAK	No need. I've just remembered. (Takes a camera from box.) Here's an X-ray camera. (Holds it up and takes picture.) There. (Takes plate from back of camera and holds it up to light.) It's all right. Your temperature's quite normal. (Replaces camera and plate in box and starts to shake BUBBLE vigorously.)
BUBBLE	What are you doing?
SQUEAK	Shaking the thermometer down, of course.
BUBBLE	Well don't. Try and get it out somehow.
SQUEAK	See if you can cough it up.
	(BUBBLE coughs rather genteelly.)
	Perhaps if I give you a pat on the back it would help. (Picks up crutch and swings it back.)
BUBBLE	No! (Gives an extra loud cough. Whirr from ORCHESTRA and glass crash off R.) There.
SQUEAK	You've broken it.
BUBBLE	Never mind. Let's have a look at your head now.
SQUEAK	All right. (Takes the bandage off like a hat.)
BUBBLE	No, no, do it properly. Put it on again and I'll unwind it.
	(SQUEAK replaces bandage, BUBBLE undoes pin fastening it and starts to unwind it, twirling

1 - 2 - 32

	SQUEAK round and round until he goes twirling off R., while he backs to L. with the bandage stretched across the stage. Enter KING R. with a bundle of forms.)
KING	Lord High Chamberlain, there's a bandage floating round the palace, why?
BUBBLE	I was just attending to Squeak's wounds, your Majesty.
KING	What are you talking about? What's the Lord Low Chamberlain got to do with it?
BUBBLE	Well, he's on the other end of the bandage.
KING	No, he's not.
BUBBLE	Not? Good gracious, where's he got to, then?
	(Enter SQUEAK L. still twirling. He cannons into BUBBLE, who is knocked into KING and all fall in a heap.)
KING	What's going on here? What are you playing at, Squeak?
SQUEAK	I'm having my head examined.
KING	Well, if you're going to behave like that I should think you need to. However, never mind that now, I've a job for you two. I understand that my daughter's going round with that young Durden lad and I won't have it.
BUBBLE	Tut-tut, of course not, sire.
KING	So in future both of you will accompany her constantly when she's out and if any commoner wishes to address her he must apply for my permission by filling in one of these forms. In triplicate, naturally.
BUBBLE	Naturally.
SQUEAK	What about us? Do we have to fill in a form to speak to her?
KING	No, no. My purpose is to preserve the dignity of the royal house. It's all a matter of etiquette.
SQUEAK	Ah, I see. What's etiquette?

KING	Bubble, I see we shall have to explain.
BUBBLE	Yes, your Majesty.

MUSIC 33 ETIQUETTE

KING and BUBBLE	If you're wanting a job (Weekly wage, seven bob) In a palace rich and gay, You must never forget That correct etiquette Is your duty if you would stay.
SQUEAK	If a shine I must get On an old coronet, What's the stuff to use for it?
BUBBLE	Though some Vim I have tried, Also Omo and Tide, What I recommend is spit!
KING	You must not show your surprise When we have kippers for our tea.
BUBBLE	You must tell most awful lies Because it's called Diplomacy.
KING	If a Dame or a Lord Goes a bit overboard You must never be upset; Out of mind, out of sight Ev'ry action is right –
ALL	That is palace etiquette.

(Close traverse tabs slowly. When they are closed, fly out cloth.)

SQUEAK	Will you please tell me how I'm expected to bow When my breeches are so tight?
KING	You must cover the tear With a nonchalant air Till you sew it up at night.
BUBBLE	It's essential that you Know the right thing to do, Whether standing or on your knees; You must get in your head

	Certain things that are said, Such as 'Thank you', and even, 'Please'.
KING	Serving meals you must not dream Of standing round awaiting tips.
BUBBLE	It's considered great esteem To serve the royal fish and chips.
SQUEAK	If the weather is damp And there's only one gamp Surely somebody gets wet!
KING	You must not lose your grip!
BUBBLE	Simply stand there and drip!
ALL	That is palace etiquette!
	BLACKOUT
	(Open traverse tabs.)

1 - 3 - 35

ACT ONE

Scene Three - THE MARKET PLACE

(MUSIC 34. Full set. Gay market setting. Cut-out of local Corn Exchange or Town Hall, etc. at back of rostrum. Steps down in C. of rostrum. Wing L. and wing R. representing market booths. LIGHTS very dim to open. A NIGHT WATCHMAN (one of CHORUS) enters R. on rostrum with a lantern on a pole and comes down steps.)

NIGHT WATCH Five o'clock of a fine morning and all's well.
Five o'clock of a fine morning and all's well.

(He goes off L. and the LIGHTS begin to come up slowly to give the effect of dawn. A cockerel is heard crowing (Grams.). The CHORUS, as market folk, enter singly and in couples, singing slowly and sleepily at first and then in a more lively way as the song progresses and the LIGHTS continue to rise.)

MUSIC 35.   MARKET DAY

CHORUS Five o'clock on a sunny morning;
Fine good weather has come to stay.
We have brought our goods to market
At five o'clock on a market day.

(DAME, JACK and SIMON enter L. on rostrum and come down.)

DAME, JACK and SIMON Six o'clock on a sunny morning;
Fine good weather has come to stay.
We have brought our goods to market
At six o'clock on a market day.

(BUBBLE and SQUEAK enter R. on rostrum and come down.)

BUBBLE and SQUEAK Seven o'clock on a sunny morning
King and Princess now come this way.

(KING, yawning rather, and PRINCESS enter R. on rostrum and come down.)

KING and FELICIA Even royalty can rise early,
At seven o'clock on a market day.

	(LIGHTS are now up to full.)
ALL	Eight o'clock on a sunny morning; Fine good weather has come to stay. We/they have brought our/their goods to market At eight o'clock on a market day.
KING	Dear me, how time flies. But now to more serious matters. Certain undesirable commoners have been addressing themselves too freely to our royal daughter. In future, therefore, everyone wishing to speak to her Highness must apply for my permission on the forms obtainable from the Lord Chamberlains.
	(CHORUS makes sounds of dissent.)
JACK	Well, of all the silly ideas.
KING	Enough! We have spoken. You may all of you get about your business.
	(CHORUS go off L. and R., grumbling.)
	(To JACK.) And as for you, young man, I would remind you that it is market day, the day on which your family's debts must be paid.
DAME	That's all right, Kingie. Jack's going to look for a job and we're going to raise the rest of the money on our dairy produce stall. We'd better hurry and get it ready, Simon. It's eight o'clock and not a dairy maid or a milk churn emptied.
	(DAME and SIMON go off R.)
KING	We will return to the palace, my dear.
FELICIA	(with a quick look at JACK) No, I think I'll stay, Father.
KING	I see. Very well, my child, by all means. Chamberlains, remain with her Highness and see my instructions are properly carried out.
BUBBLE and SQUEAK	Yes, your Majesty.
	(BUBBLE places himself at PRINCESS's R. and SQUEAK at her L.)

1 - 3 - 37

KING	And that, I think, should settle that. Goodbye, my dear.
	(He bows to PRINCESS, who curtseys to him. BUBBLE and SQUEAK bow and keep their heads down. KING turns and looks at JACK, who nods curtly. KING sniffs and turns to strut haughtily away and walks tummy first onto SQUEAK's bowed head.)
	Oupff! Squeak, I do wish you'd get a softer head.
	(Exit R. BUBBLE and SQUEAK straighten up.)
BUBBLE	Strange, I always thought you were very soft in the head.
JACK	Squeak.
SQUEAK	Yes?
JACK	Can I speak to the Princess?
SQUEAK	Now the King's gone, yes - go ahead.
BUBBLE	Certainly not! What are you thinking of, Squeak?
SQUEAK	Love. I was in love myself once.
FELICIA	Were you, Squeak?
SQUEAK	Yes, she was only a greengrocer's daughter, but she certainly knew her onions. Ah me, how we used to cry together over those onions. But I lost her to another, so it all turned out for the best in the end.
FELICIA	Oh, not for you.
SQUEAK	Well, you should have seen the greengrocer's daughter.
	(BUBBLE starts weeping copiously.)
FELICIA	Ah, there, there, Bubble.
BUBBLE	It's all so sa-a-ad. (Blows nose loudly.)
OTHERS	(comforting him) Now, now, don't cry, etc.
SQUEAK	You'll let Jack talk to the Princess now, won't you, Bubble?
BUBBLE	(stopping crying suddenly) No

OTHERS	No?
BUBBLE	No.
SQUEAK	Meanie. I needn't have bothered to make all that up. Ah well.
BUBBLE	If the young man wishes to speak to her Highness, he must apply for the King's permission in the proper way. (Proffers forms.)
JACK	But he'll never give it, so that's absurd.
FELICIA	No, it isn't. Squeak, ask that gentleman if he would care to borrow a pencil.
SQUEAK	Would you care to borrow a pencil?
JACK	No.
FELICIA	Good, then lend him one.
	(SQUEAK shrugs and takes out a stub of pencil which he gives to JACK.)
JACK	But I don't -
FELICIA	(taking forms) Now pass him these forms.
	(SQUEAK does so.)
JACK	But what's the -
FELICIA	Of course, you'll take the completed forms to the King right away, Bubble?
BUBBLE	Yes indeed, your Highness.
JACK	Ah, I see. Bend over a minute, Squeak.
	(SQUEAK bends over so that JACK can write on his back.)
BUBBLE	But they must be completed in triplicate.
FELICIA	Certainly. Tell him in triplicate, Squeak.
SQUEAK	In triplicate.
JACK	In triplicate? Very well.
	(SQUEAK starts to giggle and wriggle.)
	Hey, keep still.

1 - 3 - 39

SQUEAK	I can't, you're tickling me in triplicate.
JACK	That's it.
SQUEAK	(straightens up) Thank goodness it wasn't quadruplicate.
JACK	(giving BUBBLE forms) Here you are, Bubble.
BUBBLE	Thank you, we'll take them straight to the King. Wait here till we bring back the answer. (Moves a few paces R. then stops.) No talking, of course, while we're gone.
JACK and FELICIA	No, of course not.
	(BUBBLE and SQUEAK exeunt R. JACK and PRINCESS laugh.)
JACK	(whispering) If we can't talk, do you think it's all right to whisper?
FELICIA	I think it's all right to talk.
JACK	(whispering) Oh no, that would be cheating. I tell you what, though -
	<u>MUSIC 35.</u> NOT OUT LOUD
JACK and FELICIA	Let's sing a little song in whispers. Our love is underneath a cloud So we mustn't try to rush, We must sing with lots of hush, And not out loud. Though people try to separate us, Our heads are gory but unbow'd. If we stand as close as this We can give a little kiss - But not - out - LOUD! Ssh!
	(Exeunt L. on tiptoe. Enter SIMON R., carrying a milking stool and a pail.)
SIMON	Daisy! Daisy! Oh, where can she have got to? (Sits on stool.)
	(JOAN jumps on L.)
JOAN	Hello. What are you doing?
SIMON	Milking a cow. Well, I mean, I would be only I've

	lost her. What are you doing?
JOAN	Looking for Father. I've lost him.
SIMON	What! Then he might be lurking waiting to pounce somewhere! Anywhere! Here!
	(DAISY enters R., behind SIMON and gently touches him with her head.)
DAISY	Moo!
SIMON	(jumping in the air and falling over) Aah! He is! He touched me! I can't move! I can't get away! (To audience.) Help, please!
AUDIENCE	Steady, Simon!
SIMON	(rises confidently, pulling himself up and looking very tough) Giant, eh? I'll deal with him. What's a measly little Giant? (Turns.) Oh, Daisy, it's only you. Where have you been, you naughty girl?
	(DAISY whispers in his ear.)
	Oh, I see. She's been to the florist's to buy some underwear.
JOAN	Underwear at the florist's?
SIMON	Yes, cowslips. Now, milking. (To JOAN.) Do you know how to milk a cow?
JOAN	No, but I'd like to learn.
SIMON	It's very simple. This is the milking stool, which is used for sitting on while the cow is being milked.
	(DAISY nods. Rear half sits on stool and the front half on the rear and crosses one leg over the other.)
	No, no, no, Daisy. Not by you, by me.
	(DAISY rises reluctantly. SIMON puts stool in front of DAISY's back legs.)
	It goes here and I -
	(DAISY kicks over stool.)
	Naughty, Daisy. (Picks up stool and replaces it.

	It goes here and I - well, go on.
	(DAISY shakes head.)
	That's all right then. It goes here and I sit on it.
	(He is about to sit and DAISY slides stool to one side and looks airily innocent when he sits on ground.)
	Funny.
	(He rises and is about to sit again. DAISY slides it back to its original position, but SIMON turns and sees this just in time and clamps a hand down on the stool.)
	Caught you! (Sits triumphantly.) Next, I place the pail here, (Places it under DAISY.) to catch the milk which comes out when I squeeze the squeezers, like this. (Starts milking.)
JOAN	I see.
SIMON	Well, I wish I did. There's nothing coming through.
JOAN	Why don't you try it like this then? (Works DAISY's tail like a pump handle.)
SIMON	Oh no, that's no good.
	(Milk spurts out.)
	Wait a minute, though, it is.
	(Milk stops.)
	There. You can stop pumping now. That'll be the lot.
JOAN	(stops pumping) But you've only got about half a pint there.
SIMON	I know, but Daisy doesn't have a very good yield.
	(DAISY snorts, kicks over bucket and goes off R. with head held disdainfully high.)
JOAN	Simon, you've upset her.
SIMON	And she's upset the milk. (Mops it up with a handkerchief and wrings it into pail.) This'll never do for gold top now. I'd better go and catch

	her. You never know what she might do in this sort of mood.
JOAN	I'll do it, I'll be quicker than you. (Jumps R.)
SIMON	Thanks. And Joan -
JOAN	(jumping back) Yes?
SIMON	I - er - I lo - (Clears throat.) I lo- (Lamely.) like you.
JOAN	Good. I 'like' you, too. Just the way you 'like' me. (She jumps off R.)
SIMON	Ooh, coo! (Gambolling round stage and ending up D.L.) I'm in like! I'm in like! I'm in like!
DAME	(off L.) Mind your backs, please. Mind the way there. (Enters L. pushing a stall on which there are a brace and bit; a pot of blue, a pot of red and a pot of orange paint; a paint brush; two sets of butter patters; a slab of butter; a bowl marked 'EGGS'; a hen; a bottle of milk; two little pullovers, one a Fair Isle; a slab of cheese.) Here we are, the one and only Dame Durden's Dairy Produce stall. Come along, now's your chance. I'm not here today and gone tomorrow. I shall be gone today. So, before I say bye-bye, come and buy, buy. Now then, you, sir -
	(SIMON turns, in a reverie.)
	Oh, it's you, Simon.
SIMON	Eh? Oh, hullo.
DAME	I'm looking for some customers.
SIMON	(looking off R.) There's somebody coming now. Oh no, he's the pieman.
DAME	Yes, he looks a bit pi.
	(Enter PIEMAN R. carrying a tray with five pies on it, one rather green and one breakable.)
PIEMAN	Pies, lovely fresh pies. Who'll buy my fine pies?
DAME	Here, this is our pitch.
PIEMAN	Can't help that. Pies, lovely fresh pies.

DAME	If you're going to stay here, you'll have to buy something.
PIEMAN	I don't want to buy anything.
DAME	Yes, you do. (Signals to SIMON behind PIEMAN's back.) You want to buy something to make some more pies with.
	(They move down on either side of him.)
PIEMAN	I shan't until I've sold these.
DAME	But you won't be able to sell those. (Picks up a pie.) Look at this one - stale. (Throws it off.)
PIEMAN	Hey -
SIMON	(picking up the green pie) Look at this one - mouldy. (Throws it off.)
PIEMAN	Stop -
DAME	(taking another) This one's too soft. (Throws it off.)
SIMON	(taking another) And this one's too hard. (Throws it off.)
	(Both pick up breakable pie.)
DAME	And as for this one -
	(It breaks in the middle.)
SIMON	It's coming to pieces.
	(They throw off the two halves.)
DAME	Now we can do business. You'll need some milk.
PIEMAN	(sulkily) Oh, very well. Give me some pasteurised.
DAME	Pasteurised? Certainly. Here's one pint -
	(Picks up milk bottle and throws it across PIEMAN's face to SIMON, who catches it.)
DAME and SIMON	Past-your-eyes!
	(SIMON plonks bottle on PIEMAN's tray.)

PIEMAN	I've changed my mind, I'll have jersey instead.
SIMON	All right, jersey milk. (Puts the plain pullover on top of the bottle.)
PIEMAN	Hey, that's not fair, I'll -
SIMON	Oh, Fair Isle jersey. (Changes the plain pullover for the Fair Isle one.)
DAME	Now how about some eggs? (Shows bowl.)
PIEMAN	But they're all broken.
DAME	Well, they're sort of instant scrambled.
PIEMAN	No, thank you.
DAME	Then how about a do-it-yourself egg-laying kit?
PIEMAN	A do-it-yourself egg-laying kit? What's that?
DAME	(picking up hen) This.
PIEMAN	Oh, no.
DAME	Then have some cheese and make some cheese pies.
PIEMAN	What sort of cheese have you got?
SIMON	(holds up slab of cheese) Cheddar.
PIEMAN	Well, I'd prefer Gruyère.
SIMON	Gruyère? Certainly. (Picks up brace and bit and starts to bore cheese.)
PIEMAN	No, perhaps Stilton would be nicer.
SIMON	Stilton. (Puts down brace and bit and starts to streak cheese with blue paint.)
PIEMAN	Or maybe Cheshire.
SIMON	Cheshire. (Starts to paint cheese with orange paint.)
PIEMAN	No, no, Dutch.
SIMON	Dutch. (Starts to paint it red.)
PIEMAN	No, I think I'll have Cheddar after all.
SIMON	(flings paintbrush down and throws cheese off angrily) We haven't got any.

DAME	Butter, then. Two pounds of best butter for the gent.
	(She and SIMON get behind stall and pat the butter vigorously with the patters. They get in each other's way and have a sword fight with the patters, which develops into playing pat-a-cake. <u>MUSIC 36.</u> This gives them the idea of using them as castanets and they break into a Spanish dance, ending up on either side of PIEMAN, bringing their feet down with a final stamp on his feet.)
DAME and SIMON	Olé!
PIEMAN	Ahaaohh! I'm fed up with this. I'm going.
DAME	No, wait. I tell you what, we'll let you have the lot, stall and all. Here, take it, take it.
PIEMAN	Take it?
DAME	Yes, take it.
	(PIEMAN starts to push it L. eagerly.)
	Er - hm, there's just <u>one</u> little thing - how much are you going to pay us?
PIEMAN	Nothing. You said take it, so I'm taking it.
	(Exit L. with stall.)
DAME	Ooh, the cheeky thing.
	(Enter JACK R.)
JACK	Hullo, Mother, how did the sale go?
DAME	My boy, we were the victims of a take-over bid. Have you got a job?
JACK	So far I'm afraid not.
DAME	Then we're ruined, ruined!
SIMON	Oh, cheer up, Mrs Durden, something's bound to turn up.
	(Enter DAISY R.)
DAISY	Moo!
DAME	Daisy! That's it. Oh no. We couldn't. But we

	must. No, no. Yes, yes. It's the only way.
JACK and SIMON	What is?
DAME	(drawing them aside and whispering conspiratorially) We shall have to sell Daisy.
JACK and SIMON	(astonished, full voice) Sell Daisy!
DAME	(whispering) Ssh! I want to break it to her gently. Leave me alone with her for a bit.
JACK	All right, Mother, but I don't like the idea.
SIMON	Neither do I.
DAME	Do you think I do? But how else can we raise the money?
JACK	(sighs) I don't know. Come on, Simon.
SIMON	Yes, just a minute.
	(DAISY is scratching herself with a rear leg and much to her astonishment SIMON kisses her tenderly, then joins JACK to go off L.)
DAME	Daisy, there's something I wanted to say to you, dear. You see -
	(DAISY rubs her head affectionately against DAME.)
	Oh dear, this doesn't make it any easier. The fact is, Daisy, we haven't any money left and so we've got to ask you to help us.
	(DAISY looks up enquiringly.)
	How? Well, that's the nasty bit. We thought we might raise some money if we - if we sold you.
	(DAISY shakes her head, very distressed. DAME strokes her gently.)
	Oh, we don't want to get rid of you, don't think that; but you're the only asset we've got left. Please say you understand.
	(After a pause DAISY nods miserably.)

Thank you, Daisy. (Hugs her.) And it may only be for a little while. As soon as things get better I promise we'll buy you back. But whatever happens, I'll never forget you.

MUSIC 37. MEMORIES

I have so many things to remember;
Such lovely things, as daffodils in May,
The sound of wavelets softly kissing pebbles,
And a great log crackling on a winter's day.
But of all the memories that may escape me -
And as years go by I'm bound to lose a few -
I swear with all my heart, so please believe me,
I will always remember you.

(Enter JACK L., carrying a rope halter. MUSIC continues under this dialogue.)

JACK Mother, I've brought Daisy's halter for you.

DAME Oh dear, I don't think I can face selling her myself. Please, Jack, do it for me.

JACK Of course, Mother.

DAME Ah, there's a good lad. And be sure and get a good price for her. We don't want to let our Daisy go for next to nothing.

JACK I'll do my best. (Puts halter round DAISY's neck.) Ready, Daisy?

(DAISY nods unhappily.)

DAME Goodbye, Daisy. (Embraces her.) Goodbye.

(MUSIC comes up a little. DAME stands D.L., looking after DAISY as JACK leads her off R. Just before they go off DAISY stops and turns to wave a mournful hoof. DAME waves back. They go off. DAME sighs and goes off sadly D.L. MUSIC out. PRINCESS enters U.R. followed rather breathlessly by BUBBLE and SQUEAK.)

BUBBLE Your Highness, wait, please.

SQUEAK Yes, I'm losing my breath.

FELICIA And I'm losing my patience. Will you please

	go away?
	(GREEN FLASH L. <u>MUSIC 38.</u> Enter DEMON L. BUBBLE and SQUEAK clutch each other in fear.)
DEMON	Madam, I'll rid thee of these two.
SQUEAK	Aah! Help! We only had a few. I'm going.
BUBBLE	Yes, and so am I.
FELICIA	No, wait, I've changed my mind.
SQUEAK	Oh my! Well, can't you change it back again?
BUBBLE	No, duty calls, we must remain. (With great trepidation.) Who are you? I don't know your face.
SQUEAK	I think he's come from outer space.
DEMON	Begone! My patience with thee's flown. I'd with the Princess speak alone.
BUBBLE	Then first, unless you've royal kin, This form in triplicate fill in. (Offers forms.)
DEMON	A plague upon thy pesky form! (Knocks the forms flying.)
SQUEAK	Oh, look! He's started up a swarm.
BUBBLE	(running round picking up the forms) Well, really! Oh dear, such a state.
DEMON	I bade ye go, now 'tis too late, And since ye have prov'd so defiant Ye must thy chance take with the Giant! Here he doth come!
	<u>MUSIC 39.</u>
GIANT	(off L.) Fee-fi-fo-fum!
BUBBLE	Help for the Princess!
SQUEAK	And us too!
BOTH	Help! Help!
DEMON	I charge ye, cease this hue!

1 - 3 - 49

(Makes a magic pass with his hands and they are suddenly rendered silent and immobile.)

GIANT (off L.) Fee-fi-fo-fum!
To steal the Princess here I come!

(FELICIA screams and runs R. but DEMON seizes her and drags her to L.)

DEMON Nay, thou'll not 'scape my fell design!

(GIANT is heard laughing evilly off L. and his huge hand and arm appear L. to drag FELICIA off screaming and protesting.)

GIANT (off L.) Got you, my bird! She's mine! She's mine!

DEMON (laughs) 'Tis well. Now with the cow I'll deal
And thus young Durden's fate shall seal.
(To BUBBLE and SQUEAK.)
So shout and clamour as ye will,
Ye'll find that it avails ye nil!

(He releases them with a magic pass and laughs again. BLACKOUT. DEMON goes off. LIGHTS UP. BUBBLE and SQUEAK come to life, a little befuddled.)

BUBBLE and SQUEAK Ooh, where are we?

BUBBLE I feel most odd. Just as if I'd had a blackout. Now what were we doing? Ah yes, shouting for help for her Highness. Her Highness! Where is her Highness? Where is she? Where is she?

(CHORUS run on L. and R.)

CHORUS What is it? What's the matter, etc.

BUBBLE The Princess has been stolen!

CHORUS The Princess stolen!

(Enter KING U. R.)

KING Stolen? What do you mean, stolen?

SQUEAK Well, she's been and gone and gone.

BUBBLE And there was an extraordinary man here, too.

1 - 3 - 50

SQUEAK	And he's been and gone and gone, as well.
KING	An extraordinary man?
	(Enter JACK D.R.)
JACK	What's happened? What's everybody shouting about?
KING	There he is! Seize him!
BUBBLE	No, not that extraordinary man, sire.
KING	Don't try to shield him! Seize him!
	(BUBBLE and SQUEAK shrug and do so.)
	What have you done with my daughter? Tell me this instant where have you hidden her?
	(JOAN jumps on L.)
JOAN	Stop! He hasn't got the Princess.
	(ALL wheel round.)
KING	Then who has?
JOAN	My father, the Giant!
ALL	The Giant!
	(BUBBLE and SQUEAK release JACK. <u>MUSIC 40.</u>)
KING	Oh, this is dreadful. I'll give any reward that anyone cares to name, if only they'll rescue my daughter.
JOAN	No use, your Majesty. The Giant will keep her locked up in his castle in the sky. No one can get there unless, like me, they can jump as high as the clouds.
KING	Then can no one find her?
JOAN	No one.
JACK	(stepping forward) I can.
KING	Foolish youth. You can't even find a job, let alone a Princess.
	(CHORUS laugh.)
JACK	Laugh if you will, but somehow, I swear, I'll find her.

(Sings.)
Wherever she may be, I swear
I'll find her;
In fire or water, earth or air
I'll find her.
Though my way lies through the vale of tears,
Though I travel to the furthest spheres,
Though I have to search a thousand years,
I'll find her,
I'll find her,
I'll find her!

BLACKOUT

(Close traverse tabs. Fly in Scene Four frontcloth.)

ACT ONE

Scene Four - ON THE WAY HOME

(Country road frontcloth or tabs. If cloth is used open tabs as soon as convenient. <u>MUSIC 41.</u> GREEN FLASH L. and DEMON enters L. carrying bag of gold.)

DEMON At last, at last, my triumph's nigh!
Young Jack will soon come passing by
Despondent that the cow's not sold,
So I shall offer him this gold -
Which I have cast a spell upon -
And by the time he's homeward gone
Each golden coin will be a bean -
A subtle dig at Evergreen!
But ere I dupe him with this pelf
'Twere best that I disguise myself.

(Takes out a book labelled 'LETT'S DEMON'S DIARY' and opens it.)

And here the very means are shown -
'How to become an aged crone.
See page twelve.'
(Flips over a few pages.)
'First create a nose,
Then round the head a shawl dispose;
Next drape the limbs with tatter'd cloak
And change the voice to frog-like croak.
Six magic words this trick will do,
Help'd by a magic pass or two.'
Well, what could simpler be than that?
I'll do it in ten seconds flat.
(Making magic passes.)
Abracadabra! Sesame!
An old hag's nose evolved be!
(Produces a rose and flings it away in disgust.)
It was not rose, but nose, I said.
(Makes more passes and produces false nose.)
That's better. Now then, for my head.
(Making more passes.)
Cadabra-abra! Presto-hey!
A woollen shawl send me, I pray!
(A wooden ball bounces on from L.)

Confusion! Not a wooden ball!
(Kicks it off L. angrily and a woolen shawl comes
on from there, hitting him in the face.)
Ah, well. Now I'll my last need call.
 (Making more passes.)
Dabra-abraca! Hocus-poke!
Make no mistake, I want a cloak,
So nothing but a cloak create.
(A large bag labelled 'COKE' drops beside him on
a wire from flies.)
This wretched book is out of date!
(Throws book off.)
'Tis cloak, not coke, I'm asking for.
(The coke returns to flies.)
My diction's clear enough, I'm sure.
(A cloak descends from the flies, enveloping him
and he fights his way out.)
Ten thousand curses! Ah, I'm clear.
Now can the aged crone appear.
(He puts on cloak, false nose and shawl.)
There. Now the voice a wheezy crack.
(Emits a strangled croak and speaks in a hoarse
voice, assuming a bent posture.)
And just in time, for here comes Jack.

(JACK enters R. rather despondent, leading
DAISY.)

JACK
Well, now we're really in the stew.
I've had no luck in selling you.
So home I s'pose we'll have to go.

(DAISY nods delightedly.)

JACK
What Mother'll say I just don't know.

(DEMON steps forward and speaks in his
croaking voice.)

DEMON
Good day, young sir, I wonder now
If you, perchance, would sell that cow?

JACK
You mean, you'd buy her?

DEMON
                            Aye, I would.

(DAISY draws back, rather hostile.)

JACK	Come here, Daisy, now now, be good. She's shy, you know.
DEMON	Some old cows are.
	(DAISY is outraged by this remark and advances menacingly on DEMON.)
JACK	Oh dear, I think you've gone too far. Daisy, stop! Don't get in a rage.
	(DAISY stops between them and JACK whispers to DEMON.)
	She's rather touchy re her age.
DEMON	Ah, to be sure, the sweet young thing.
	(DAISY is partly mollified.)
	Now what price did you hope she'd bring? Is this enough? (Holds up bag of gold.)
JACK	What is it?
DEMON	Gold.
JACK	(taking bag and looking inside it) I say!
DEMON	Well, what's your answer?
JACK	(shaking DEMON's hand) Sold!
	(DAISY shakes head vigorously.)
	Yes, Daisy dear, the bargain's struck; I knew that you would bring us luck. Though, while to get the gold I'm glad, To part with you is very sad.
	(DAISY hangs her head sorrowfully.)
	Farewell, old friend. No, please don't cry. Give me your hoof and say goodbye.
	(DAISY gives her R. forehoof for JACK to shake.)
DEMON	Come on, good cow. (Aside.) Aha! I've won! At last the Fairy's day is done! Now my star is most luminant. But first this scraggy ruminant Unto the Giant I will take;

	A nice pot roast for him she'll make.
DAISY	(outraged) Moo! (Puts her head down and paws ground.)
DEMON	No! 'Twas a joke, there there, good cow - I didn't mean it - gently -
	(DAISY charges and knocks him off L. and follows after him.)
	Ow!
JACK	Oh dear, I hope they'll be all right. Ah well, this gold should save our plight.
	(He starts to go off L. MUSIC 42. FAIRY hurries on R. also disguised as an old crone, but still adjusting her shawl and cloak.)
FAIRY	I think I've got here rather late. Wait, young man - I mean - (Assumes hoarse voice and makes herself very bent.)
	Young man, wait!
JACK	Another aged dear, well, well.
FAIRY	Oh - haven't you a cow to sell?
JACK	Not now, good dame.
FAIRY	Why not, I pray?
JACK	I have just sold her.
FAIRY	Lackaday!
JACK	To one who like yourself was dress'd.
FAIRY	Like me?
JACK	In fact, I would have guess'd Almost your twin.
FAIRY	My sister dear! (Aside.) Methinks I scent some mischief here. 'Tis Pestblight's work. (To him.) Tell me, kind sir, Did you a good price get from her?
JACK	(showing bag of gold) Why yes, all this.

1 - 4 - 56

FAIRY Good gracious me.
(Peers inside bag. Aside.)
Ah, yes - the Demon's trick I see.
Well, I another trick do know.
(To him.)   From this your fortune's bound to grow.

JACK I must show Mother my surprise.
I bet she'll scarce believe her eyes.

FAIRY I think you're right.

JACK Goodbye.

FAIRY Farewell.

(Exit JACK L. FAIRY removes disguise and throws it off. Close traverse tabs. Fly out cloth. MUSIC 43.)

Oh, I could stamp and scream and yell!
To think how nearly I have lost;
But 'twill the Demon dearly cost.
Unto the Durdens' house I'll hie,
Invisible to mortal eye,
And use his guile for my own means -
I'll give that Demon Pestblight beans!

BLACKOUT

(Open traverse tabs.)

1 - 5 - 57

ACT ONE

Scene Five - DAME DURDEN'S COTTAGE -

and Grand Transformation to -

THE GARDEN

(Half-set to open. Cottage backcloth or flats, in front of rostrum. Cottage wings L. and R. These wings should be booked with movable centre flaps, which at present are fixed to the sections running onstage. L. wing has a stove in front of it. Shelf above stove which has on it a tea pot, a cup and saucer and a spoon, a glass and a saucepan. Wing R. has practical window in the section running D.S. Kitchen chair L.C.
Enter DAME L. in her nightdress, with paper curlers in her wig.)

DAME Dear, dear, it's getting very late. Where can Jack be? I'll have a cuppa while I'm waiting for him.   (Pours out a very black-looking liquid into cup.)   Hm, rather strong - must have got stewed. Well, I'll get stewed as well.   (Pours the contents of the cup (Guinness) into the glass and sits in chair.)   I do like my tea with a nice head on it.   (Drinks.)   I hope Jack's got a good price for Daisy. If there's a bit over when we've paid the rent we might buy a new stove and a fridge. And I would like a new dining room suite. I mean, orange boxes are all very well, but they're not really contemporary, are they? (Rises and lifts teapot lid.)   Pity, empty. Never mind   the dining room suite then - I'll have three dozen bottles of tea instead.

(Enter JACK L.)

JACK Mother!

DAME Oh, Jack, my boy, hurry up and show me how much you got, I'm dying of thirst.

JACK All this, Mother.

(Gives her the bag of gold and the weight of it nearly overbalances her.)

DAME		Good gracious! Were you paid in pennies?
JACK		No, better than that.
DAME		Silver?
JACK		Gold!
DAME		Gold! (Leaps to her feet.) Oh, how simply stupenderful! I hardly dare look at so much lovely wealth. (Opens bag and quickly closes it again.) Aah! Blinding! All that gold's gleaming away just like a lot of shiny beans. Beans. (Looks in bag again.) It is beans! Not gold at all! It's beans!

(MUSIC 44. Enter FAIRY R. in a diaphanous cloak of invisibility.)

FAIRY (aside) I thought to look she'd ne'er decide.
Now she must throw the beans outside,
And hid by this from mortal een
I'll aid her in the task unseen.

DAME Explain this instant what this means,
There's nowt in here but blooming beans!

JACK No, no, it's gold, I'll swear it is,
Here, let me see. (Looks in bag.)
          Well, what a swizz!

DAME Our Daisy sold for scarlet runners!
Such stupidness just leaves me stunners.
Oh, Jack, how could you?

JACK   But I'm sure
This bag had gold in it before.

DAME Bang go my hopes of stove and fridge,
Of bottl'd tea -

(FAIRY is getting a little impatient and taps DAME on arm with wand. Knocks on wood block. DAME flicks at the place irritably.)

          Was that a midge?
What can we do?

(FAIRY opens window invitingly.)

JACK   I just can't say.

DAME		Well, first I'll throw these beans away.

(FAIRY nods in agreement. DAME moves L.)

Into the dustbin they shall pop.

(FAIRY is horrified and raises her wand, MUSIC TING which stops DAME, to FAIRY's relief.)

DAME   I can't, it's full up to the top.
And waste not want not, as 'tis said,
At least by them we can be fed.

(Picks up saucepan to put beans in. FAIRY shakes her head vigorously.)

I can't be bothered.

(Puts down saucepan. FAIRY shows her relief and points to window.)

          Ah, I know.
The fire.

(FAIRY very perturbed as DAME bends to put beans in the grate.)

JACK   No use, it's out.

DAME   Oh, blow!

(FAIRY fans herself in relief.)

Then on the mantel, that's the place,
In mem'ry of your sad disgrace.

(JACK looks very miserable. FAIRY raises wand again, MUSIC TING, and points imperiously to window.)
No, such remembrance I'd not bear.

(DAME moves across to window, FAIRY helping to draw her there.)

MUSIC 45.

The only place for them is - there!

(Throws them out of window, to FAIRY's great relief.)

Now, while we can, let's go to bed.

(Enter SIMON R. holding the bag of beans and

1 - 5 - 60

	rubbing his head.)
SIMON	I say, these hit me in the head.
	(Gives bag to DAME, who stamps her foot with frustration as FAIRY does likewise.)
DAME	Oh no!
SIMON	What's up?
DAME	You silly scamp! 'Twould truly make a fairy stamp.
	(FAIRY nods in agreement.)
	I just don't want them. (Thrusts bag into SIMON's hand.)
SIMON	Nor do I. Where shall we put them?
	(FAIRY impatiently wrests bag from his hand and holds it by window. MUSIC WHIZZ.)
	Here, they fly!
JACK	They seem'd to jump up from his hand.
SIMON	Ah, jumping beans, I understand.
DAME	(crossing to window, taking bag from FAIRY's hand and throwing it out) Then they can jump right out again. (Shuts window firmly and dusts hands.) And jumping back will be in vain.
FAIRY	At last! Now for my magic art.
	(Waves wand. MUSIC 46. BLACKOUT. WHITE FLASH. FAIRY removes cloak. LIGHTS UP. SIMON has fainted into DAME's arms.)
DAME	That lightning gave me quite a start. (Turns and sees FAIRY and drops SIMON with a cry of surprise.) Is this another jumping bean?
FAIRY	I am the Fairy Evergreen.
SIMON	(sitting up) A fairy, coo!
JACK	A fairy, eh?

DAME	Fairies don't often come this way.
SIMON	(rising) I had one once, belong'd to me,
	But she liv'd on a Christmas tree.
DAME	It's rude to ask, but p'r'aps you'd tell,
	What brings you so far from your dell?
FAIRY	Thy son's within my fairy care.
	For him I've plann'd a future rare.
	(To JACK.)
	So if in fortune's sun ye'd bask,
	Go, be equipped for thy task.
	Ye other mortals, too, begone,
	Thine eyes must never look upon
	The wonders that shall here be wrought!

(Waves wand. <u>MUSIC 47.</u> BLACKOUT. JACK, DAME and SIMON exeunt. Chair and stove are struck. WHITE SPOT on to FAIRY.)

Now to those beans so dearly bought –
A potent spell I'll cast on each,
Till they the very heavens reach!

(FAIRY turns U.S., waves wand with an upward movement and cottage cloth is flown, or the flats are struck. She then points to L. and R. wings and the movable centre flaps are moved across to cover D.S. flaps. On the sides now showing are a garden wing R. and the cottage exterior L. CHORUS as BEANS are discovered on rostrum, and in the ballet which follows the FAIRY brings them to life to help her create the beanstalk, which rises U.C. from behind a low wall or rockery cut-out set on front of rostrum. Beanstalk should be foliage concealing a rope ladder and is pulled up by means of a thin but strong nylon line over a pulley attached to a batten in flies. Garden cut out at back of rostrum. U-V lighting effects could be used for the transformation and ballet. At the end of the ballet, when the beanstalk is fully grown, CHORUS go off and LIGHTS UP to full.)

The work is done and with the dawn
The mortal folk are hither drawn.

(Enter DAME and SIMON sleepily L. SIMON now

	in a nightshirt.)
DAME	Well, I have had a lovely sleep.
SIMON	(yawning) Yes, so have I, extremely deep.
	(They see beanstalk.)
DAME	Good gracious! How did that get here?
SIMON	It's magic!
FAIRY	Aye, but do not fear. The wonder's yet but half begun; For now, behold! here comes thy son.
	(JACK is led on from L. by some of CHORUS. He is magnificently arrayed in armour.)
DAME	My boy, you really look a charmer.
SIMON	Where did you get such shiny armour?
FAIRY	Look up the beanstalk to the sky, And tell me, Jack, what ye descry.
JACK	(looking up) The top is wreath'd about with cloud, But now I see, within that shroud, The turrets of a castle fair.
FAIRY	Aye, 'tis the Giant doth live there. Would'st dare to scale that lofty peak?
JACK	(leaping forward to climb beanstalk) Would I?
DAME	No, wait, Jack, hear me speak. It's much too dangerous by far, Please stay and comfort your old ma.
JACK	No, Mother, I can't break my vow; I'm sworn to find the Princess now.
	(FAIRY signals to R. and CHORUS GIRL enters with a sword. **MUSIC 48.**)
FAIRY	Thy courage earns its own reward. (Giving sword to JACK.) Take thou this wond'rous power'd sword. Whoe'er of fear shows not one quake This sword invincible will make, No matter what the danger be.

	Climb then, thy fortunes wait on thee!
	(DAME weeps on SIMON's shoulder.)
JACK	I will. No, Mother, dry your eyes, I go to where my future lies. And with high hopes I do begin That I the highest prize may win!
	(MUSIC surges up as JACK starts to climb beanstalk. Others wave to him.)
	CURTAIN
	(CURTAIN rises on a tableau with JACK as far up beanstalk as possible.)
	CURTAIN

ACT TWO

Scene Six - THE TOP OF THE BEANSTALK

(MUSIC 49. ENTR'ACTE.
Full set. Cut-out rock formation piece at back of rostrum with cut-out top of the beanstalk growing above it in C. Behind rostrum are steps leading up to a small platform, about 15in x 15in on a level with top of rock piece and just to L. of beanstalk. Wing L. and wing R. representing cloud-topped rocks. LIGHTS DIM to open so that beanstalk is seen silhouetted against sky. MUSIC playing as curtain rises. DEMON discovered by L. of beanstalk, looking down it. As he calls up the elements in the following, the CHORUS enter as balletic representations of them.)
MUSIC 50. INCANTATION. (Can either be sung or just spoken to music.)

DEMON
Slow step by step young Jack draws near,
But he shall never set foot here.
Come, Hail! Come, Frost! Come, Lightning Flash!
Come, Rain! Come, Wind! Come, Thunder Crash!
This beanstalk's topmost point encage
With all thine elemental rage;
Make thou this peak a lowly tomb
And send Jack crashing to his doom!

(To the accompaniment of THUNDER ROLLS (Orchestra), WIND NOISES, LIGHTNING FLASHES the CHORUS commence a ballet, during which the DEMON suddenly points to the beanstalk and JACK appears climbing up. Under DEMON's direction CHORUS try to tumble JACK off and prevent him from getting down onto rostrum. They do not succeed and he presses forward, but they make a sudden rush at him and nearly manage to push him over the wall, but JACK remembers his sword just in time and draws it. CHORUS immediately fall back and rush off L. and R.)

Curst be! The lad has too much pluck,

	And so his sword doth bring him luck. But I'll not yet my hopes abate, I'll cause the Giant to seal his fate!
	(DEMON goes off L. LIGHTS UP to full.)
JACK	(sheathing sword) That was a near thing. That storm blew up so suddenly it almost knocked me off the beanstalk. I wonder what other dangers there are up here?
	(DAISY bellows off R. and we hear JOAN's jumping sound. JACK draws sword and faces R.)
	What's that?
	(DAISY gallops on R., with JOAN holding onto her tail.)
JOAN	Daisy, wait! You're going the wrong way.
JACK	Daisy! (Sheathes sword.)
JOAN	Jack Durden!
	(She lets go of DAISY's tail and DAISY, released so suddenly, cannons into JACK and almost knocks him over.)
JACK	(laughing) Steady, Daisy!
	(DAISY rubs her head happily against him. JACK strokes her.)
	Well, I never thought I'd meet you up here.
JOAN	She was brought up here by a wicked Demon and now the Giant wants her for his supper. I'm trying to hide her, but she will keep running back to the castle. I say, how did you manage to jump up here?
JACK	I didn't. I climbed up that beanstalk.
JOAN	Well, you'd better climb down it again before the Giant finds you.
JACK	I'm not afraid of him. But I tell you what, Daisy could escape down it.
JOAN	That's a jolly good idea. Come on, Daisy.
	(She tries to push her to beanstalk, DAISY

	protesting volubly and straining back.)
JACK	It's all right, if you just ask her nicely she'll go, won't you, Daisy?
	(DAISY almost nods, but looks at beanstalk, shakes head, turns swiftly and runs off R.)
	Hey! Come back!
JOAN	(laughs) Well, at least she's running away from the castle. Don't worry, I'll hide her. You just get back down the beanstalk.
JACK	No fear, I came up here to rescue the Princess and I'm not going down again till I have.
JOAN	But - but -
JACK	It's no use butting. I'm very determined. Also, I'm in love.
JOAN	Oh, are you? So am I. It's rather nice, isn't it? Shall we compare notes?
JACK	What sort of notes?
JOAN	Musical notes, of course.
	MUSIC 51. OUR LOVE
JACK	I am in love with a pretty lady, Pretty lady, pretty lady, And I believe that my pretty lady Is in love with me. Some sunny day when our trials are over We will tread the path of clover; I'll steal away with my pretty lady To eternity.
JOAN	I'm in love with somebody who makes me sort of stammer, Not the slightest glamour - Can't recall his grammar - Not the sort of hero from a classic melodrammer - Yet I'm all aflutter when he passes by. Though I must confess that he is just a little dim, I know he's in love with me and I'm in love with him. There are many times when I could hit him with a hammer -

	Yet I know I'll love him till the day I die.
	(Repeat verses singing against each other. JACK and JOAN go off L.)
DAME	(off, yodelling) Ur-a-liar-tee! (Appears climbing up to L. of beanstalk.) Ur-a-liar-tee! (Reaches platform.) We've made it, we're at the top! (Nearly topples backwards.) Oops! We were nearly at the bottom again. Forward, men! Ur-a-liar-tee!
	(Jumps down onto rostrum and BUBBLE appears on platform.)
BUBBLE	Ur-a-liar-tee!
	(DAME jumps D.S., BUBBLE onto rostrum and SQUEAK appears on platform.)
SQUEAK	Ur-a-liar-tee!
	(DAME moves forward, BUBBLE jumps down onto stage, SQUEAK onto rostrum and SIMON appears on platform. All are in Alpine costume and are roped together, SIMON having the rope round his ankle. He carries what looks like a rolled-up tent and DAME a small pouch haversack.)
SIMON	I'm-a-liar-too!
	(He is almost pulled off platform onto rostrum as others move forward, DAME moving round to L. so that they end up in a line D.S. across the stage. As they move.)
	Hey, wait a minute!
DAME	What's the matter, Simon?
SIMON	I think my end of the rope has slipped.
DAME	Well, I told you not to tie it in a slip-knot. Now if we're going to help Jack, I suppose we'd better find him.
BUBBLE	Oughtn't we to establish a base camp to operate from first?
DAME	Very well, let's explore for a suitable spot. Off we go.

2 - 6 - 68

(SIMON puts 'tent' down. DAME turns to move L. BUBBLE to move U.S., SQUEAK D.S., and SIMON to R., so that they all pull against each other.)

BUBBLE We seem to be slightly at variance with one another.

DAME Yes, we'd all better go a different way.

(BUBBLE turns to go L., SQUEAK to go R. DAME crosses below BUBBLE to go R., and SIMON crosses below SQUEAK and DAME to go L. DAME trips and falls over the rope between SIMON and SQUEAK, which brings them all down.)

You know, it would be much simpler if you'd all follow me.

(They rise. DAME moves forward to R., BUBBLE wheels round to follow her, stepping over the rope between SIMON and SQUEAK. SQUEAK follows on behind BUBBLE, also stepping over the rope.)

SIMON (still facing L.) Well, I would if I could see you. Where are you?

(The others moving forward tauten the rope and he is pulled over. DAME has circled round to L. and is now just U.S. of SIMON.)

DAME Come along, Simon. This is no time to rest. Get up and follow me, dear.

(She helps him to rise, but this jerks back SQUEAK and pulls him over, which pulls BUBBLE over and then the DAME.)

BUBBLE Mrs Durden, do you think there's a rather more powerful force of gravity up here?

SQUEAK I think it's this rope.

DAME There, why didn't we think of that before? Aren't you a clever Squeak? Let's try exploring without it.

(They undo rope and SQUEAK gathers it up and throws it off R.)

Now then.

(All rise and step forward so that BUBBLE and SQUEAK meet face to face R., and DAME and SIMON likewise L.)

ALL   Pardon.

(BUBBLE and DAME step to their L., as SQUEAK and SIMON step to their R.)

So sorry.

(BUBBLE and DAME step to their R., SQUEAK and SIMON to their L.)

My fault.

(ALL step to their L. and continue round so that SQUEAK and SIMON meet face to face U.S., and DAME and BUBBLE D.S.)

DAME   I think it's just overcrowded up here.

(ALL turn D.S.)

I tell you what, let's pitch the tent. Where is the tent, Simon?

SIMON   (crossing R. to it)   Here.   (Throws it to her.)

DAME   Well, I want you to pitch it, dear.   (Throws it back to him.)

SIMON   Pitch it? Right.   (Throws it to her feet.)
           There, I've pitched it.

DAME   Not that kind of pitch. When you pitch a tent you put it up not throw it down. You two unroll it and we'll show him.

(BUBBLE and SQUEAK unroll 'tent', which turns out to be a long roll of ironing.)

BUBBLE   Rather a strange tent.   (Picking up a pair of bloomers.)   Where does this piece go, Mrs Durden?

SQUEAK   (picking up some corsets)   Or this piece?

DAME   Eh? Simon, you silly thing, you've brought the week's ironing.

SIMON	Oh, sorry. (Picking up a large nightie.) Never mind, your nightie's large enough for a -
DAME	Simon! Kindly unhand my garments at once. You'd better chuck the whole lot back down the beanstalk.
	(BUBBLE, SQUEAK and SIMON gather up the things and throw them over the wall.)
	We shall have to sleep rough. Anyway, I can cook us a meal if we start a fire. Who brought the firewood?
SQUEAK	I did. (Gives her one stick of firewood.)
DAME	Is that all?
SQUEAK	Yes.
DAME	We'll have to make do with a snack then. Have you got a match to light it with?
SQUEAK	No, when you're camping you're supposed to rub two boy scouts together.
DAME	Ah yes, of course. Fortunately I just happened to bring a couple with me. (She brings out from haversack two boy scout dolls and rubs them together vigorously.) Where's the food, Simon?
SIMON	(looking towards beanstalk) I left it to come up on its own.
DAME	What sort of food is it, then?
SIMON	Flour.
	(A bag of flour rises on the beanstalk, pulled up on a wire threaded through beanstalk and over a concealed pulley.)
DAME	Ah, self-raising, of course.
	(Bag of flour goes down again.)
SQUEAK	Self-lowering, too.
SIMON	We don't seem to be very good at any of this, do we? I mean, we can't put up a tent.
DAME	Or light a fire. (Throws dolls off.)

2 - 6 - 71

BUBBLE	Or explore.
SQUEAK	Or even yoddle very well.
OTHERS	Yoddle?
BUBBLE	It's yodel, not yoddle, you noddle.
SQUEAK	And it's noodle, not noddle.
BUBBLE	It tiddle.
SQUEAK	It tid.
BUBBLE	Oh, twaddle.
DAME	Don't quaddle - I mean, quarrel. It'll only lead to trouble, Bubble. If he wants to yoddle, let him. In fact, let's all yoddle.

<u>MUSIC 52.</u> YODELLING

ALL	Ev'ry Saturday night at home, When we were very young, We yodelled for our supper, And yodelling songs were sung.
SIMON	Father had a growling bass And sang with all his might, 'Yodel-de-a-yodel-de'.
ALL	Ev'ry Saturday night.
BUBBLE, DAME and SQUEAK	Ev'ry Saturday night at home, etc.
BUBBLE	Uncle had a tenor voice And reach'd fantastic height - Yodel-de-a-yodel-de.
SIMON	Yodel-de-a-yodel-de.
ALL	Ev'ry Saturday night.
DAME and SQUEAK	Ev'ry Saturday night at home, etc.
DAME	Sister had an alto voice, The lowest thing in sight - Yodel-de-a-yodel-de.
BUBBLE	Yodel-de-a-yodel-de.
SIMON	Yodel-de-a-yodel-de.

2 - 6 - 72

ALL	Ev'ry Saturday night.
SQUEAK	Ev'ry Saturday night at home, etc. Mother was soprano, but Her throat was rather tight - Yodel-de-a-yodel-de.
DAME	Yodel-de-a-yodel-de.
BUBBLE	Yodel-de-a-yodel-de.
SIMON	Yodel-de-a-yodel-de.
ALL	Ev'ry Saturday night. Ev'ry Saturday night at home, etc. We would sing together, for To sing was our delight.
SQUEAK	Yodel-de-a-yodel-de.
DAME	Yodel-de-a-yodel-de.
BUBBLE	Yodel-de-a-yodel-de.
SIMON	Yodel-de-a-yodel-de.
ALL	Yodel-de-a-yodel-de. Ev'ry Saturday night.
DAME	There now, who could object to a lovely drop of yoddeling like that?
	(MUSIC 53. LIGHTNING FLASH, CYMBAL CRASH and LIGHTNING jumps on R. to behind DAME, holding menacingly a long jagged sword shaped like a lightning flash.)
	Dear me, I think there's going to be a storm.
	(CYMBAL CRASH and HAIL jumps on L. to behind SIMON. HAIL has extended fingernails painted with black and white bands to suggest hailstones, with which she threatens the back of his neck.)
SIMON	Yes, a hail storm.
	(CYMBAL CRASH and FROST jumps on R. to behind BUBBLE. FROST has a sharp pointed icicle at the end of each hand with which she menaces BUBBLE.)
BUBBLE	Brr - I think I can feel a touch of frost.

2 - 6 - 73

                (WIND NOISE, CYMBAL CRASH and WIND jumps on L., behind SQUEAK and flutters the draperies at the end of her arms at him.)

SQUEAK   There's a nasty wind getting up.

                (ALL turn in towards their respective menacers.)

ALL   Aah!

                (They start to run, closely followed by their elements. The following business was designed for an auditorium with aisles running up and down each side and with a transverse aisle at the front and another about half way up; also with entrances at the L. and R. sides and L. and R. at the back, all of which were joined by passages out of sight of the audience. Obviously Producers may have to re-arrange the business to suit their own auditoriums. The important thing is to keep the audience continually surprised and therefore never to leave them without something happening either on the stage or in the auditorium or both. The directions given here, by the way, are given from the audience's L. and R. when in the auditorium. SQUEAK and WIND run U.S. and round in a clockwise circle. BUBBLE and FROST run in anti-clockwise circle outside them. SIMON and HAIL run straight across and off R. HAIL proceeds round back of stage to wait off U.L. DAME and LIGHTNING run straight across below SIMON and HAIL and exit L. to proceed to an entrance at R. back of auditorium. SIMON runs on U.R., and realises he is without HAIL when he reaches C. He stops, panting heavily, looks round, creeps over to R., goes stealthily off below U.R. wing and almost immediately pops his head on above it. Walks confidently onstage over to U.L. where he stops and turns to look back a little puzzled. HAIL jumps on behind him U.L. and jabs him with her nails.)

SIMON   Waaahh!

                (They circle anti-clockwise and exit U.L. to proceed to an entrance at R. side of auditorium. At the same moment SQUEAK and WIND appear D.R.,

2 - 6 - 74

                        run to catwalk, over it and into auditorium to run up R. hand aisle and mark time when they meet DAME and LIGHTNING who rush in at entrance at R. side of auditorium and run across a transverse aisle to exit at L. side of auditorium. DAME proceeds to entrance at L. back of auditorium. LIGHTNING waits in passage. As soon as DAME and LIGHTNING have passed them SQUEAK and WIND run forward again, but meet BUBBLE and FROST who emerge from entrance at R. back of auditorium. SQUEAK and WIND wheel round to run back, but again have to mark time, and so do BUBBLE and FROST as SIMON and HAIL run on from entrance at R. side of auditorium, turn R. and go down L. aisle, until SIMON reaches ORCHESTRA pit and turns round not knowing what to do. HAIL stands against wall and politely indicates 'after her'. SIMON bows his thanks, runs past her, she follows on and they go out through exit at L. side of auditorium to proceed to entrance at R. back of auditorium. As soon as SIMON and HAIL have passed them, SQUEAK, WIND, BUBBLE and FROST run forward D. R. aisle. SQUEAK and WIND turn L. at the ORCHESTRA pit and run along front aisle, at the end of which SQUEAK tries to climb onto stage. WIND helps him up. He doffs his cap to her and starts to run U. S., then remembers his manners and turns to help her up. BUBBLE and FROST have run over catwalk and onto stage and are running round in clockwise circle. SQUEAK and WIND run outside them in anti-clockwise circle. DAME runs on from entrance at L. back of auditorium down to transverse aisle, then stops realising she has lost her pursuer.)

DAME   Coo-ee! Bet you can't catch me-ee!

                        (LIGHTNING jumps out from entrance at L. side of auditorium and jabs DAME with sword.)

                        Waahh!

                        (They run across transverse aisle and go off at R. side of auditorium to proceed to stage and enter D. L. SIMON and HAIL run on at entrance at R.

2 - 6 - 75

                    back of auditorium and run down R. aisle and up over catwalk onto stage to D.C. where SIMON stops.)

SIMON   Stop!

(ALL stop.)

I can't go on any more, I'm too frightened.

(LIGHTNING, WIND and FROST move menacingly towards him.)

Frightened! Of course.   (To audience.) Help, please!

AUDIENCE   Steady, Simon!

SIMON   Ah, that's more like it. (Turns very confidently to the elements, pulls a terrible face and waggles his hands in his ears at them.) Yah!

(LIGHTNING, WIND, FRONT and HAIL run screaming off D.R.)

DAME   Oh, Simon, you brave lad.

SIMON   It was nothing. It takes a lot to scare me, you know. (Swaggers L., stops suddenly seeing something and turns tail and flees off R.) Aah! Help! Save me! Save me!

DAME   What's the matter with him all of a sudden?

<u>MUSIC 54.</u>

GIANT   (off L.)   Fee-fi-fo-fum!

ALL   Aah! (They run R.)

DAME   Don't bother to answer that question.

(Exeunt R. and GIANT enters L. He is a two-headed, three-legged GIANT, wearing built-up boots, rather shaggy wigs with pads in to give more height, large false ears and hands and shaggy beards and moustaches. He carries a key-ring holding several large keys on the R. of his belt. HEAD A is rather fierce-looking, HEAD B rather sad-looking.)

2 - 6 - 76

HEADS A and B	Fee-fi-fo-fum. I smell the blood of an Englishman. Be he alive or be he dead, I'll grind his bones to make my bread.
HEAD B	But I don't like bread. It's so fattening.
HEAD A	Nonsense, I'm very fond of bread. Especially white bread and nobody makes better white bread than Englishmen.
HEAD B	Oh no, they give my half of the stomach colly-wobbles.
HEAD A	Colly-wobbles! Bah! Don't take enough exercise, that's the trouble.
HEAD B	I daren't. I just can't stand up to much exercise.
HEAD A	Of course I can. I'll have some now. Arms flinging out and in - go! Out! In! Out! In! (GIANT does the exercise until HEAD B hits himself in the face with the L. hand.)
HEAD B	Ow!
HEAD A	Marking time on the spot - go! Left, right, left, right, left, right, left. Centre, centre, centre, centre. (GIANT does this exercise.) There, fit as a fiddle! (Hits himself on chest with R. hand. HEAD B splutters and coughs.)
HEAD B	Then I'm a bit out of tune.
HEAD A	No, I'm not. Just worked up a nice little appetite. (Smacks lips.) Where's that Englishman? I'm sure I smelt one here a minute ago. (Sniffs.)
HEAD B	All I can smell is beans.
HEAD A	Beans? Ridiculous! There aren't any beans here. (Sees beanstalk.) What's that?
HEAD B	Beans.

2 - 6 - 77

HEAD A	Well, I don't like it. I don't like it at all.
HEAD B	I do. I'm very fond of beans.
HEAD A	But how did it get here? I smell dirty work.
HEAD B	(sniffs) I don't. I smell sulphur now. I suppose that wretched Demon's lurking somewhere ready to jump out just when one isn't expecting him.
	(GREEN FLASH L. and DEMON enters L. and bows low. HEAD B is startled. DEMON carries a harp.)
	Aah! There, you see? What did I say?
DEMON	Greetings, Sir Giant.
HEAD A	How do?
HEAD B	Good day.
	Can't you arrive with less fussation? You give my heart such palpitation.
DEMON	Mayhap this gift will prove a balm To bring thy shatter'd nerves some calm. (Holds out harp.)
HEAD B	I doubt it, still -
HEAD A	Now, now, don't carp. What is it?
DEMON	Why, a magic harp, That plays most sweetly on its own. List to its rare and dulcet tone. Play, harp. (Nothing happens.) Play! (It plays one note and then stops.) A slight hitch. (Gives it a bang.) Oh, fudge! (Harp plays (grams)). Ah, there, it's started with a nudge.
	(As harp continues to play, GIANT shows his delight. When it has stopped -)
HEAD A	Well, ain't that nice?
HEAD B	Yes, very gay.
DEMON	(giving harp to GIANT) Whene'er you bid it, it

	will play. It hath another power too. It doth with envy all imbue, So that to steal it they do try; But cannot, for the harp will cry, 'Awake! Awake! O, master mine!' If touch'd by any hand save thine.
HEAD B	I must say that the thing has charm, A built-in burglar proof alarm.
HEAD A	For catching Englishmen, I swear, 'Twill prove a simply splendid snare.
DEMON	(aside) And therein my real purpose lies. Jack might have 'scap'd the Giant's eyes Had I not plann'd this fatal trap. (To GIANT.) I'm glad you're pleased.
HEAD A	No end, old chap, I revel in these magic toys.
DEMON	Then I will leave you to its joys.
HEAD A	Oh, must you go?
DEMON	I fear so, aye. Farewell, Sir Giant. (Bows.)
HEAD B	Ta-ta.
HEAD A	Bye-bye.
	(Exit DEMON L.)
HEAD B	Well, I suppose he's not too bad really.
HEAD A	Certainly not. Jolly good bloke. Pity he's not a Giant. I bet he wouldn't turn up his nose at a nice juicy Englishman.
HEAD B	Oo-er. I'm getting the colly-wobbles again.
HEAD A	And I'm getting fed-up. It's a disgrace to the family. Look at Mother, she never had colly-wobbles. What a fine figure of a Giantess she was.
HEAD B	Ah, yes - those three dear grey heads.
HEAD A	And what about Father? A magnificent fellow. Four heads and five legs. Ah, they don't make Giants like those nowadays.

MUSIC 55. GIANTS AIN'T WHAT THEY USED TO BE

BOTH	Giants ain't what they used to be; Giants are slipping, I fear.
HEAD B	Once I had two hundred cakes for tea.
HEAD A	Wash'd down with ten gallons of beer.
HEAD B	Once I gave people much cause to grouse -
HEAD A	I'd pull up their trees and I'd sit on their house!
HEAD B	Now I get hysterics if I see a mouse!
BOTH	I ain't what I used to be.
HEAD A	Giants ain't what they used to be; Giants are slipping, I vow. Once if they charg'd me an entrance fee That started a terrible row; If 'You must pay for your ticket,' they said, I gave them a biff on the boko instead; Now I pay for admission at so much per head! I ain't what I used to be.
HEAD B	Giants ain't what they used to be; Giants are slipping, it's true. Once on a time you were frighten'd of me, But now I am frighten'd of you. I was a terrible tyrant for years; I bred in the populace 'orrible fears; Now if people look crossly, I burst into tears - I ain't what I used to be.
	(DANCE.)
BOTH	Once on a time I was fully fed On fat little children of Leatherhead; Now I wish I were playing at Dorking instead - I ain't what I used to be.
	(The above lyric can be altered to suit local place names or the following can be used:)
	Once on a time I was fully fed On fat little children all locally bred; Now I wish I'd been born as a midget instead - I ain't what I used to be.
	BLACKOUT (Close traverse tabs. Fly in cloth.)

ACT TWO

Scene Seven - OUTSIDE THE GIANT'S CASTLE

(If a cloth is used open tabs as soon as convenient to reveal the main entrance of the castle painted in C. with a brass plate inscribed 'G. BLUNDERBORE, ESQ', beside it. Above the entrance is written -

'Abandon hope all ye who enter here,
We're frying tonight any who appear.'

There is a notice to the L. of the cloth, pointing off L., which reads, 'TRADESMEN'S ENTRANCE'.

DAISY runs on R. and stops in C. and looks round.)

DAISY   Moo!   (Starts to walk L.)

DAME   (off at L. back of auditorium)   Ooh-ooh!

(DAISY is startled and runs off L., then peers cautiously on again. DAME enters in auditorium. HOUSELIGHTS UP. DAME makes her way through audience.)

Coo-ee! Now where's everybody got to? In fact, where have I got to? I suppose it's part of Giantland, but I must say you look very measly little giants to me. I like my Giants in the large economy size.

DAISY   (comes on stage, very excited)   Moo!

DAME   (to one of the audience)   I beg your pardon? Did you say something?

DAISY   Moo!

DAME   That's funny, you sounded just like my old cow, Daisy. You're not an old cow, are you?

DAISY   Moo!

DAME   (looks up)   Goodness gracious! It is Daisy! (Running to catwalk.)   Please forgive me, I must go.

(HOUSELIGHTS OUT as she runs onto stage and embraces DAISY.)

	Daisy, my love, however did you get up here? Oh, I'm so pleased to see you I could just sing for joy. In fact, I will! (CONDUCTOR's name:) are you up the beanstalk, dear?
CONDUCTOR	Yes.
DAME	Oh good, and all your friends have brought their instruments up with them, I see. That pianist of yours must be a very strong lad. I wonder if you could give me some music for a song I invented just this very minute?
CONDUCTOR	Certainly.
DAME	Thank you.

MUSIC 56. MOO, MOO, MOO

I've a cow call'd Daisy,
And she'd win any prize,
With legs on all four corners
And two great big eyes.
Daisy's got a message,
For me to give to you –
'Drinka pinta milka day
and moo, moo, moo!'

(DAISY joins in on last 'Moo'.)

Oh, you clever girl, Daisy, you've learnt it already. You'd never believe I'd just invented that, would you?

(DAISY shakes head.)

Daisy, how could you? Anyway, you'll never believe what I'm going to do now. I'm going to ask all those pigmy Giants down there to sing it with us. (Calling off.) Hey, Bill, let down the portcullis, will you?

(The Songsheet comes down in C. designed as a portcullis.)

Thank you. Right, (CONDUCTOR), off we go. (Lets audience sing for a little.) No, no, no, that's not good enough, is it, Daisy?

(DAISY shakes head.)

	Perhaps you misunderstood. I want you all to sing. Thank you, (CONDUCTOR.)
	(Audience sing song a desired number of times with suitable encouragement from DAISY and ad-lib from DAME.)
	Oh, very nice. I've got another surprise for you now.
	(Enter BUBBLE, SQUEAK and SIMON at R. side of auditorium. HOUSELIGHTS UP. They make their way to catwalk.)
SIMON, BUBBLE and SQUEAK	Dame Durden!
DAME	Ooh, that was a surprise for me.
SIMON	We've been looking for you all over the place.
DAME	Then you've found me just at the right moment. I was just going to ask the children to come up here and sing, so now you can help them up.
	(Ad-lib while the children are helped onto stage and while they sing, and then while BUBBLE, SQUEAK and SIMON help them down and DAME encourages rest of the audience to sing. When they have all returned BUBBLE, SQUEAK and SIMON get onstage. HOUSELIGHTS OUT.)
	Very good, and before we go and find Jack there's just time to sing it once more altogether - so really let yourselves go. Thank you, (CONDUCTOR).
	(Fly songsheet and close traverse tabs as song is sung for last time. Fly cloth. On last few bars all exit L. waving to audience.)
	BLACKOUT
	(Open traverse tabs.)

ACT TWO

Scene Eight - THE GIANT'S KITCHEN

(Kitchen cutout at back of rostrum. A large table C. in front of rostrum. GIANT's chair behind table, or a chair seat built up on rostrum. To R. of chair the GIANT's club. Against rostrum U.L. a wing with practical door, opening onstage, marked 'EGG CUPBOARD'. U.R. against rostrum a similar wing with door marked 'STORE CUPBOARD'. Steps down in front of these doors. D.R. a wing with a large oven in front of it, with practical door and two holes with covers in the top. D.L. a wing with practical door opening onstage, labelled 'LARDER'.
FELICIA discovered chained to rostrum at R. of table. Chains held together with large padlock.)

MUSIC 57. LOST LOVE

FELICIA
A single tear is shed in darkness,
A single cry that tells my pain.
The dreams I cherish'd
Are lost and perish'd -
The light of hope is dimm'd again.
The chains I wear cannot be broken;
No key unlocks my prison door;
But though they chain me,
Love can sustain me,
Though love is prison'd in my heart for evermore.

(JOAN jumps in cautiously L.)

JOAN (putting fingers to lips)   Ssh!

FELICIA Why? There's nobody here except me.

JOAN Oh, yes there is.

(Enter JACK L.)

FELICIA Jack!

JACK Felicia! I was afraid I might arrive too late to save you.

FELICIA But you couldn't have got here much sooner. I haven't been here very long myself.

JOAN		Not in Giant time, but time moves much more slowly up here than it does on Earth.
JACK		Well, it's moving quickly enough for me. I must get you out of these chains and away before the Giant gets back.
SIMON		(off L. in a gruff voice) Fee-fi-fo-fum!
JOAN and FELICIA		Too late!
JACK		(drawing sword) Well, I'm ready for him.
JOAN		(pushing JACK off R.) No, quick, Jack, in here, and take him by surprise.

(She and JACK exit R. Enter SIMON L. sitting on BUBBLE and SQUEAK's shoulders with his legs dangling over DAME's shoulders. This, however, we do not see, as SIMON wears a voluminous cloak which covers the others so that only their feet show.)

SIMON   Fee-fi-fo-fum - I - er, I - er -

DAME   (opening cloak in front of her face and whispering) I smell the blood.   (Shuts cloak.)

SIMON   Oh, yes. I smell the blood - here, keep still.

BUBBLE   I can't, I'm suffocating.

SQUEAK   So am I.

SIMON   Well, can't you suffocate standing still? I'll fall if you keep jigging about. Now, where was I?

DAME   (opening cloak again and whispering heavily)   I <u>smell</u> the <u>blood.</u>   (Shuts cloak.)

SIMON   That's right. I smell the blood - look out!

(They all collapse.)

JACK   (off R.)   Stand back! I'll get him while he's fallen over.

(Runs on brandishing sword, followed by JOAN. They stop short as they see the others struggling out of cloak.)

Mother!

JOAN	Simon!
FELICIA	Bubble and Squeak!
SQUEAK	Old Uncle Tom Cobleigh and all, Old –
BUBBLE	Squeak, this is no time to give a recital.
JACK	(sheathing sword and helping them up) What are you all doing here pretending to be a Giant?
DAME	We came to help you, my boy. We thought it would be easier to get in here like that.
SIMON	(rising and rubbing behind) I found it a jolly sight harder.
JOAN	Oh, poor Simon. But it's not getting in here that's difficult, it's getting out again. Father may be back any minute.
DAME	Well, he won't take us by surprise. We left Daisy outside keeping cave.
JACK	Good. Now, how can we get Felicia out of these chains?
JOAN	Well, the Giant's got the only key to the padlock, but he always has a little nap before his supper. You might be able to steal it from him then.
JACK	Good idea. Then all we need is the Giant.
DAISY	(off L.) Moo! Moo!
DAME	Aah! There he is!
SIMON	No, that was Daisy. I recognise the moo.
DAME	Of course it's Daisy. She's warning us! The Giant's here!
SIMON	The Giant! Ooh-er. (Faints into DAME's arms.)
DAME	Simon, this is no time for the vapours. Oh, now what are we going to do?
JOAN	You must hide, quickly! Leave Simon to me, Mrs Durden. You go into the larder.
DAME	Right. (Drops SIMON and runs to larder.)
JOAN	Jack, see if you can fit into the oven. Bubble, you go

2 - 8 - 86

	into the store cupboard, and Squeak into the egg cupboard.
SQUEAK	Couldn't I go into the store cupboard? I don't like eggs.
DAISY	(off L. more urgently) Moo! Moo!
SQUEAK	I'll get to like them.
	(They hurry to their hiding places. SQUEAK shuts his door.)
JOAN	(kneeling beside SIMON, patting his wrists, etc.) Simon. Simon, my love, speak to me.
SIMON	W-Where am I?
JOAN	In the Giant's kitchen.
	(SIMON faints again.)
	Oh, what can I do?
DAME	(pointing to audience) Ask them to help.
JOAN	(to audience) Help, please!
AUDIENCE	Steady, Simon!
SIMON	(leaping to his feet) What? Where? When? How? Where's the Giant? (Shadow boxing.) I'll show him. (Almost hits JOAN.) Ooh, sorry.
JOAN	Never mind. You've got to hide somewhere. I know - down on all fours and I'll cover you with your cloak.
	(He does as she bids and she covers him.)
	Now, don't anybody come out till I give a signal. Three knocks, like this. (Knocks three times on table.)
SQUEAK	(opening door) I say, there's somebody knocking.
JOAN	Yes, me. That's the signal to come out.
SQUEAK	(coming out) Oh, we can come out, can we?
OTHERS	No!

SQUEAK	(dashing back into cupboard) Oh.
JOAN	That's what the signal will be when you can. Now, all out of sight.
	(ALL shut their doors.)
GIANT	(off L.) Joan! Joan!
JOAN	Phew! Just in time. Anyway, we're ready.
	(DAISY runs on L.)
DAISY	Moo! Moo!
JOAN	Oh dear, we're not. You'll have to squeeze into the larder, Daisy. (Leads DAISY to larder and knocks once. In urgent whisper.) Mrs Durden.
GIANT	(off L.) Joan!
JOAN	Coming, Father. (Whispering.) Mrs Durden!
	(Knocks three times. OTHERS open their doors and start to come out, SIMON raises his cloth.)
OTHERS	All clear?
JOAN and FELICIA	No!
JOAN	That was a mistake, I'm trying to hide Daisy. Quick, get back!
	(JACK, BUBBLE and SQUEAK disappear. SIMON gets under cloth, DAME steps right out to let DAISY in.)
DAME	In you go, dear.
	(DAISY goes into cupboard. DAME shuts door.)
	That's it. Aah! I'm out!
GIANT	(off L.) Joan, what are you doing?
JOAN	Under the table!
	(DAME nips under table, JOAN hiding her from the sight of the GIANT who enters L. carrying harp.)
HEAD B	Didn't you hear me calling?
JOAN	Yes, Father, I –

2 - 8 - 88

HEAD A	(sniffing) I can smell Englishman again.
JOAN	(gulps) Englishman, Father?
	(GIANT moves C. HEAD A still sniffing, and puts harp on table.)
HEAD A	Yes, Englishman. In fact, Englishmen. (Pointing to SIMON.) What's that?
JOAN	Oh, he's - er - I mean, it's an occasional table.
HEAD A	I see.
	(SIMON moves L. a little.)
	It can't be a table. It moved.
JOAN	Yes, well, that's why it's called an occasional table. Occasionally it's here and occasionally it's there. (Kicks SIMON surreptitiously. In aside whisper.) Keep still!
	(GIANT sits at table and finds DAME with his feet.)
HEAD A	Ah good, you've brought the footstool in.
	(GIANTS plonks feet on DAME.)
DAME	Ow!
HEADS A and B	What?
JOAN and FELICIA	(clearing throats) Frog in my throat.
HEAD B	Both of you? You must have colds coming on. Perhaps I'd better take something as a preventative.
HEAD A	But I hate medicine.
HEAD B	No, I don't.
HEAD A	Yes, I do.
HEAD B	(thumps table with fist) I don't!
HEAD A	(does likewise) I do!
HEAD B HEAD A	(together, thumping table again) Don't! Do!
	(BUBBLE, SQUEAK and JACK open their doors, SIMON starts to emerge.)

2 - 8 - 89

JOAN and FELICIA	Go away!
HEADS A and B	What?
JOAN and FELICIA	Lovely day.
	(ALL disappear again and the three doors slam. HEAD B jumps at the noise.)
HEAD B	Oh, my nerves.
HEAD A	What was that?
JOAN	The wind. There's a storm blowing up.
HEAD A	But you just said it was a lovely day.
JOAN	Well, yes, but - er - well -
FELICIA	Wouldn't you like a little nap?
HEAD A	No, that smell of Englishman has sharpened my appetite. What is there in the larder?
JOAN	(opening the larder door a crack) Nothing much.
HEAD A	I know, what about that cow?
DAISY	Moo!
	(JOAN slams door shut.)
HEADS A and B	I beg your pardon?
JOAN	I said, 'Shoo!' I thought I saw a mouse. Anyway, the cow's not in there.
HEAD A	Of course she's not, you silly custard.
HEAD B	Custard! That's it, just the thing. I love custards.
HEAD A	Milksop.
HEAD B	Not at all. They suit my digestion. Have we enough eggs?
JOAN	Not for a custard. There's only half a gross left.
HEAD B	Is that all? Oh, do look and make sure.
JOAN	(opens and immediately shuts egg cupboard door) Yes, exactly seventy-two. I counted them.
SQUEAK	(opening door and speaking in a heavy whisper)

	Seventy-one, actually. I've just broken one.
JOAN	(slamming door) Get back!
HEAD B	Eh?
JOAN	(airily, crossing to oven) I wondered if you'd like a flap-jack.
JACK	(popping head through U.S. hole) Did you call?
	(JOAN pushes his head back and recovers hole.)
HEAD A	What did you say?
FELICIA	She didn't, it was me. I said - it's in the hall.
HEAD A	What, the flap-jack?
JACK	(popping head through D.S. hole) I'm sure I heard my name.
	(JOAN pushes him back again and recovers hole.)
HEAD A	What did you say that time?
FELICIA	I said - yes, it's a sort of game.
HEAD B	I know what I'd like to eat - bubble and squeak.
BUBBLE and SQUEAK	(opening their doors) Yes?
JOAN and FELICIA	No!
	(BUBBLE and SQUEAK disappear.)
HEAD B	Well, I only asked.
HEAD A	I'm tired of all this.
FELICIA	Tired? Then do have that little nap.
HEAD A	All right. No wait. Bring me my hen that lays golden eggs.
DAME	A hen that lays golden eggs!
HEAD A	(to JOAN) Don't sound so surprised. You know perfectly well she lays one every day.
DAME	One every day!
HEAD A	And don't keep repeating everything I say. Just go and fetch Hetty.

2 - 8 - 91

JOAN	Right away, Father. (Exit R.)
HEAD B	I say, this footstool's very lumpy. (GIANT takes feet off DAME.)
DAME	Well, really!
HEAD B	(to FELICIA) Well really, what?
FELICIA	Er - well, really I thought it was very well upholstered.
HEAD B	Yes, but not in the right places.
	(Enter JOAN R. with some sheets of music and prop hen with gold egg attached - concealed from audience. JOAN places hen in front of GIANT.)
JOAN	Here you are, Father.
HEADS A and B	Ah, my little Hetty.
HEAD A	Come along, good little hen.
HEAD B	Lay a nice gold egg for Daddy.
	(Hen cackles, (grams))
	That's it.
HEADS A and B	(stroking hen) Chuck-chuck chuck-chuck.
	(Hen's cackle ends with a little whoop. HEAD A takes egg and holds it up.)
HEAD A	There.
DAME	Cor!
HEAD B	(to JOAN) Four, did you say? Oh no, one a day's quite enough. We don't want Hetty to over-strain herself.
FELICIA	And you mustn't overstrain yourself either. You have your little nap now.
JOAN	Yes, I've brought the music for your favourite song so we can sing you to sleep.
HEAD A	Very well. No, wait. I can play myself to sleep with my new harp.
	(HEAD A puts the egg down and HEAD B stands harp upright.)

2 - 8 - 92

HEAD B	Oh, yes. Just watch this, it's marvellous. Play, harp.
	(Harp plays.)
HEAD A (to FELICIA)	Isn't that pretty?
HEAD B (to JOAN)	
JOAN and FELICIA	Very pretty. (Yawning to encourage GIANT.) And so soothing.
HEADS A and B	Yes. (They yawn.) Pardon me. (They yawn again, this time covering their mouths with each other's hands, then lean their heads against each other and begin to snore gently.)
FELICIA	(whispering) He's asleep.
JOAN	(whispering) I'll give the signal.
	(She taps softly three times. BUBBLE, SQUEAK and JACK open their doors and creep out, BUBBLE and SQUEAK to either side of DAME, who creeps out from under table on all fours. JOAN drops down to SIMON.)
JACK	(whispering) Now for that key. (Moves to GIANT and detaches keyring very carefully.)
DAME	(whispering) Help me up, you two.
	(BUBBLE and SQUEAK do so.)
	OW! Me rheumatics!
OTHERS	Ssh!
DAME	(whispering) Sorry.
JOAN	(whispering) Come on, Simon, you can come out now. (Shakes him.) Simon! (Lifts cloak.) He's gone to sleep too. Simon, wake up!
SIMON	(noisily yawning and stretching) Ah! What?
OTHERS	Ssh!
	(JACK unlocks padlock.)
FELICIA	I'm free! (Drops chains with a thud.)

HEAD A	(a beatific smile coming on his face) Um, Englishmen.
	(Everyone freezes. JACK hides keys behind his back. FELICIA hastily picks up chains and holds them as if she is still chained.)
	(Waking suddenly.) Englishmen! (Picks up club and brings it down on table with a thump.)
	(ALL utter cries of distress.)
HEAD B	(jerking awake) What? What's the matter? Oh, visitors.
HEAD A	Joan, what is the meaning of this? You said there weren't any Englishmen here.
JOAN	Well, there weren't. I mean, they've only just arrived.
DAME	Yes, and now we've got to go again.
	(They start to move L.)
HEAD A	(banging club on table) Stop!
	(They do.)
	I insist on all of you staying for supper.
SIMON	I say, isn't that nice of him?
HEAD A	Don't mention it. I'm sure you'll all taste delicious.
BUBBLE	Oh no, we might give you the colly-wobbles.
HEAD B	That's true.
SQUEAK	And then you wouldn't be able to get off to sleep again.
FELICIA	And you do want to go to sleep again, don't you?
HEAD A	No.
OTHERS	Oh, you do.
JACK	Play your harp a little.
HEAD A	Shan't.
JOAN	Then this time we will sing for you. All of us.

OTHERS	Will we?
JOAN	(distributing music sheets) Yes. This song always sends Father to sleep, that's why he likes it so much.
DAME	'Rock-a-by, Baby'. (Looks at GIANT.) Oh, very suitable.

(GIANT falls to sleep during following number, which is set in the manner of Mendelssohn.)

MUSIC 58. ROCK-A-BY, BABY

ALL
Rock-a-by, baby, on the tree top,
When the wind blows the cradle will rock,
When the bough breaks the cradle will fall;
Down will come baby,
Down will come baby,
Down will come baby, cradle and all.

Rock-a-by, baby, on the tree top,
When the wind blows the cradle will rock,
When the bough breaks the cradle will fall;
Down will come baby,
Down will come baby,
Down will come baby, cradle and all.
Rock-a-by, baby, cradle and all.

Rock-a-by, baby, on the tree top,
When the wind blows the cradle will rock,
When the bough breaks the cradle will fall;
Down will come baby,
Down will come baby,
Down will come baby, cradle and all.
Rock-a-by, baby, cradle and all.
Rock-a-by, baby, cradle, cradle and all.
Rock-a-by, rock-a-by, rock-a-by.

JOAN	(whispering) It's worked!
JACK	(whispering) Good, then let's go.
DAME	(whispering) Wait. Simon, get Daisy out of the larder.
SIMON	(whispering) Right. (Opens larder door.) Come on, Daisy.
DAISY	(coming out) Moo!

SIMON	Ssh! We've got to be very quiet, Daisy. Walk on tip-hoof.
JOAN	Goodbye. I shall miss you all.
JACK	What? You can't stay here, Joan, not now you've helped us to escape.
DAME	You must come and live with us, my dear.
JOAN	But there'll be nobody to look after Hetty.
DAME	Then we'll take Hetty, too. I rather fancied her, anyway. (Picks up hen.) Might as well have this too, while we're about it. (Picks up egg.)
JACK	And the harp. I feel I must take the harp.
	(Picks up harp and ALL start to creep L. but are arrested by a loud twang from the harp, and the sound of its voice, miked.)
HARP'S VOICE	Awake! Awake! O, master mine!
	(Hen starts to cackle (grams) and GIANT awakes. <u>MUSIC 59.</u>)
HEADS A and B	What's happening? Thieves?
	(Screams and cries of dismay from others.)
JACK	Run to the beanstalk! Run for your lives!
	(OTHERS run off in confusion and GIANT rises, picking up his club. JACK and FELICIA are left. JACK drops harp as GIANT comes round table.)
HEADS A and B	Thieves! Stealing my lovely Princess!
JACK	Quick, Felicia!
	(GIANT aims a blow at JACK, who dodges to avoid it and in doing so releases FELICIA. GIANT grabs her and JACK draws his sword.)
	Giant, release the Princess or it will be the worse for you!
HEADS A and B	What!
HEAD A	You impudent pipsqueak!
HEAD B	You beastly Princess-pincher!

2 - 8 - 96

HEAD A	I'll kill you and then eat you alive!
HEAD B	Yes, and I'll even enjoy you!
HEADS A and B	Have at you! |ажд

(GIANT thrusts FELICIA behind him and raises club in both hands. A fight ensues during which JACK is disarmed and his sword knocked U.S. Just as the GIANT is about to deliver the final blow, his attention is distracted by FELICIA moving across to get the sword. JACK leaps forward, wrests club from GIANT and hits each head a hefty blow. GIANT staggers around and collapses over table. FELICIA moves to JACK and gives him sword.)

JACK   Quick, back to the beanstalk and home!

(They go off L. <u>MUSIC 60.</u> GREEN FLASH and DEMON jumps on D.L.)

DEMON   Curses! Young Jack's escap'd once more!
But I can still my hopes ensure.

(Moves to GIANT and shakes him.)

Come, Giant, revive thyself, I say!
Th'art fit to fight another day.
Confusion! He's completely out,
Which leaves my chances much in doubt.
He <u>must be</u> to his senses brought –
I have it! Yes, a brilliant thought!
I'll conjure from my magic vaults
Some extra pow'rful smelling salts.

(Makes magic passes to floor. A bottle of smelling salts descends from flies. He shrugs and holds it under HEAD B's nose.)

Just sniff a little.

(Holds it under A's nose.)

              And you too.
Aha! They're working now.

HEADS A and B   (sneezing)   Atchoo!

(GIANT staggers to his feet.)

	Oh, what happen'd? (Puts hands up to heads.) Oh, my poor heads!
HEAD B	My nerves are really torn to shreds.
DEMON	Courage, Sir Giant, all is not lost, You yet shall make them pay the cost. (Picks up club and gives it to GIANT.) Go, swiftly to the beanstalk hie, For thence thy enemies did fly.
HEAD B	Oh, must I?
HEAD A	Yes, of course, I must; My honour's trampl'd in the dust.
HEAD B	But my head's throbbing like a drum. (Sighs and shrugs.) Oh, well. Fee-fi-fo-blooming-fum. (Exit GIANT L. DEMON moves down below tab line.)
DEMON	'Tis well! Now I to earth will float That I may o'er my victim gloat. (LIGHTS OUT except for GREEN SPOT on DEMON. Traverse tabs close behind him. WHITE SPOT R. for FAIRY as she enters R. <u>MUSIC 61.</u>)
FAIRY	Gloat not too soon then, for I vow That ye have tried me far enow. If ye continue with this strife Why then, the Giant shall lose his life And I'll thy power render nil. So, Demon, say - wilt fight on still?
DEMON	I will! For I'll ne'er frighted be By paltry threats from such as thee And in a little 'twill be shown That I the final vict'ry own! (BLACKOUT. Exit FAIRY R. and DEMON L. Tabs open and LIGHTS UP to reveal Scene Nine, if cloth is used.)

ACT TWO

Scene Nine - MEANWHILE, BACK AT HOME

(Frontcloth. A village street (or Scene Four cloth could be used), or tabs.)

KING (off L.) Crowns for sale! Who'll buy my fine crowns? (Enters L. in old and tattered robes and wearing a very patched-up crown. He carries a tray in front of him with various crowns on it.) Lovely crown jewels going cheap! Oh dear, to think that I, the last of the noble line of Umptys, should be reduced to this. Things have really come to a pretty pass. In fact, they've got worse and worse ever since everybody went up the beanstalk and that was months ago. Now I can't even afford anybody to look after the palace. My fingers are worn to the royal bone with all the cleaning. Not to mention the washing. And my clothes are so much more awkward than most people's. For instance, ermine underpants - they take hours to dry. I shall get drip-dry ones next time, but first I'll have to raise some money. That's why I'm having to sell my crowns. Ah, what memories they bring back. There, my first crown. (Holds up a small crown attached to a baby's knitted bonnet.) I wore that at my Christening. It's a little rusty where it fell in the font, but never mind. And this is my school crown. (Holds up crown attached to a schoolboy's cap.) And this one - oh, this one was a mistake. (Puts on a crown that is much too big.) I only bought it because it was going cheap in a sale, but these ready-made crowns are never the same. Of course, this is the best one. My coronation crown. (Holds up a very squashed-looking crown.) Pity the Archbishop sat on it. Still, I really was a King then. Now - well, for all the notice anybody takes of me I might just as well abdicate, except no one would notice if I did. Most humiliating. But when I was young - ah, those were the days.

MUSIC 62. THE GOOD OLD DAYS

In the good old days, I went to school -
   I was very good at schooling as a lad.
      All exams were fun to pass,
      'Cos not ev'ry boy in class
   Knew a real life King that he could call his Dad!
I knew my twice times table and could sing 'God
             Save the Queen';
I could recognize the letters and could tell you
             what they mean -
And that was pretty good, 'cos I was only seventeen,
   In the good old days.

In the good old days, I went to work
And didn't take advantage of my rank.
      Just to earn a few odd bob
      I'd take any sort of job,
   Such as Managing Director of a Bank.
I thought I'd stop my overdraft from being in the
             red,
And my pretty secretary knew math'matics, so they
             said;
But they lock'd up all the lolly, so I took the girl
             instead.
   In the good old days.

In the good old days, as time went on,
Eventually I sat upon the throne.
      After years and years when we
      Bought our things upon H.P.,
   It was nice to sit on something of our own.
But now I have to carry all the burdens of the
             State,
With Parliament and protocol and put it on the
             slate,
And Peeresses and politics and pass the buck, O
             Mate!
   For those good old days!

(During last verse traverse tabs close slowly.
Fly cloth.)

Heigh-ho! On with my sorry task.   (Moving R.)
Crowns for sale! Crowns for sale!

(Loud thump from behind tabs.)

2 - 9 - 100

BUBBLE	(behind tabs)	Ow!
KING	(stopping and turning)	What was that?
	(Another thump.)	
SQUEAK	(behind tabs)	Ow!
KING	There it is again.	
	(Thump.)	
JOAN	(behind tabs)	Ow!
KING	And again.	
	(Thump.)	
SIMON	(behind tabs)	Ow!
KING	And yet again.	
	(Thump.)	
DAME	(behind tabs)	Ow!
KING	And even yet again.	
	(Extra loud thump.)	
DAME, SIMON, JOAN, BUBBLE and SQUEAK	(behind tabs)	OW!
DAISY	(behind tabs)	MOO!
KING	Good heavens! Whatever can it be? It sounded as if it came from Dame Durden's garden. I must hurry there immediately.	
	(MUSIC 63. He starts to run on the spot. ALL LIGHTS OUT, except for a SPOT on KING.	
	Tabs open.)	

ACT TWO

Scene Ten - DAME DURDEN'S GARDEN

(Set as in the latter half of Scene Five. The hen and a concealed square egg are set at foot of beanstalk.)

KING: I'm there.

(Stops running. LIGHTS UP. At foot of beanstalk we see from L. to R. JOAN, SIMON, DAME, SQUEAK and BUBBLE in a loudly protesting heap, with DAISY lying on top of them, her head to L. JACK is on R. side of the wall U.C., helping down PRINCESS who is still on beanstalk.)

Good gracious! It can't be true. (Clasps hands over eyes.)

DAME: I think we came down that last bit too quickly.

SIMON: I'm quite sure we did. I landed on my head. (Rubs head.)

JOAN: (rubbing head) So did I.

BUBBLE and SQUEAK: (rubbing their heads) And us.

DAME: And I landed on my - well, anyway, it was very painful.

(JACK jumps down from wall and helps FELICIA down.)

KING: (uncovering eyes and moving in) It is true!

FELICIA: ⎫ Father!
DAME: ⎪ Kingie!
JOAN and SIMON: ⎬ The King!   (Together.)
BUBBLE and SQUEAK: ⎪ His Majesty!
DAISY: ⎭ Moo!

JACK: (hands FELICIA across to KING and bows) Your Majesty, I have brought back your daughter from the Giant as I promised.

KING: Thank you, my boy. Oh, my child. (Embraces FELICIA.)

BUBBLE	Quick, Squeak, we must pay our respects to his Majesty. Mrs Durden, could you persuade your bovine quadruped to move?
DAME	Ye - my what?
BUBBLE	Cow.
DAME	I beg your pardon? Oh, I see - Daisy. Oi, Daisy! Cattle cake, Daisy!
DAISY	(rises hastily and scampers L. towards cottage) Moo!
DAME	That's it. In the usual tin, dear, and not too many crumbs on the carpet.
	(DAISY shakes her head and disappears L.)
BUBBLE	Now, on your feet, Squeak.
	(Rises. SQUEAK rises a little after him, facing L. DAME, JOAN and SIMON rise in same way. BUBBLE bows extravagantly to KING.)
	Your Majesty.
	(As he bows he bumps into SQUEAK's behind, which makes SQUEAK buffet the DAME's rear with his head, DAME SIMON's rear with her head and SIMON JOAN's rear with his head and all fall forward.)
	Squeak, what are you playing at?
SQUEAK	Well, I like that!
DAME	(rubbing behind painfully) I didn't. You biffed me on my beanstalk bruise.
	(They help each other to rise.)
KING	I thought I should never see you again, Felicia.
FELICIA	Poor Father.
KING	Yes, that's just the trouble, my dear. I have become very poor in all the months you've been away.
OTHERS	Months?
JACK	It's only been a day or so.

JOAN	Ah, in Giantland. But that's what I told you, time moves much more quickly down here.
KING	Anyway, the Umpty fortunes have fallen very low.
DAME	Dear, dear - the Umptys down in the dumpties, what can we do?
KING	Well, if you remember there was a trifling matter of some rent outstanding. If you could manage a little on account -
DAME	Oh, I wish we could, but -
	(Hen cackles (grams).)
	Wait a minute, we can! Hetty! What an opportune little bird.
JOAN	Yes, you'll be rich now, Mrs Durden. She lays one every day, remember.
DAME	Then she's been working overtime, I caught all these while we were coming down the beanstalk. Here, have half a dozen new laid, Kingie. (Takes some gold eggs from her haversack and gives them to KING.)
KING	That's very kind of you, but I'm not very hungry at the - GOLD!
	(More cackling.)
DAME	Hold on a jiffy. I think there's another consignment coming through.
	(Cackling gets a little desperate. ALL turn to look at hen.)
JOAN	I hope she's all right, I've never heard her like this before.
	(Cackling gets even more desperate and ends up with a cry of 'Blimey!')
SIMON	Ooh, she said something.
DAME	(taking square egg from under hen) I'm not surprised. Well done, Hetty. (Gives it to KING.) There, that should about settle everything. At last all our troubles are over.

	(GREEN FLASH L. and DEMON leaps on. MUSIC 64.)
DEMON	Not so!
	(SQUEAK jumps up on BUBBLE for protection and SIMON on DAME, but DAME and BUBBLE collapse.)
SQUEAK & SIMON	Aah!
DAME & BUBBLE	Help!
JOAN & FELICIA	The Demon!
JACK	Who?
DEMON	One who doth ruin spell for you! Know then, thy final hour has come – List who draws nigh!
	(Points up the beanstalk. DAME, BUBBLE and SIMON rise. ALL look up beanstalk.)
GIANT	(off) Fee-fi-fo-fum!
ALL	The Giant!
DAME, SIMON, BUBBLE, SQUEAK	Help!
	(BUBBLE and SQUEAK run off U.R. SIMON drags JOAN off U.L. DAME is following but stops halfway to run back and collect hen and then goes off U.L. KING pulls FELICIA D.R.)
KING	Run, child!
FELICIA	No, no, wait!
JACK	(draws sword) Yes, run or it will be too late!
	(FELICIA unwillingly allows herself to be pulled off D.R. by KING. DEMON moves in front of beanstalk.)
	I have no cause the Giant to fear, I've fought him once and still am here.
DEMON	This time thy daring is in vain. My magic shall thy limbs enchain Till thou art powerless to fight And numb and helpless wait thy plight! (Making passes with hands.)

	I charge thee, be as turn'd to stone!
JACK	(raising sword) Stand back!
DEMON	What, hath my power flown?
GIANT	(off, louder) Fee-fi-fo-fum!
JACK	Stand back, I say!
DEMON	(moving back) 'Tis true. I'm vanquish'd by the fay!
JACK	This Giant I'll deal with once for all, Both he and beanstalk down shall fall!
	(Holding sword in both hands, he strikes at beanstalk. BLACKOUT. Chopping noises, splintering sound, a great cry from the GIANT and a tremendous crash. LIGHTS UP. The beanstalk is down and GIANT is sprawled motionless over wall, or rockery. FAIRY has entered R.)
	I've done it!
FAIRY	Aye, most bravely, too!
DEMON	Curst be!
FAIRY	Begone, thy day is through! Goodness hath won as goodness should.
DEMON	My curse on ev'rything that's good. Thy triumph's pierc'd me like a knife. Who takes my evil takes my life!
	(Exit DEMON L. KING looks on D.R.)
KING	I heard a crash.
FELICIA	(looking on U.R.) I heard a shout.
	(JOAN and SIMON look on U.L.)
JOAN	What was it?
SIMON	Anyone knock'd out?
	(FELICIA enters and goes to JACK.)
FELICIA	Oh, Jack, my love.
DAME	(looking on D.L.) What's happen'd, eh?

JACK	The Giant is dead.
	(KING, DAME, SIMON and JOAN run on.)
SIMON, DAME, KING, FELICIA	He's dead? Hurray!
KING	Well done, my lad. Give me your hand. You sav'd my daughter, now our land. You well deserve a rich reward, But I, alas, can't much afford. Still, what I have, I'll give with joy. Will you have crowns or eggs, my boy?
JACK	(laughs) I thank you, neither, sir.
KING	Oh dear, I've nothing else to give, I fear.
JACK	Save that which I do most desire - Thy daughter's hand in marriage, sire; For all I did was done for love.
KING	What, must I lose my precious dove?
FELICIA	I love him, too, as he loves me.
KING	(handing FELICIA across to JACK) Then take her, Jack, and happy be.
FAIRY	Now all my hopes have come to pass.
DAME	And I have lost a son, alas! But gain'd a daughter.
FAIRY	You've gain'd two; Your long lost child's return'd to you.
DAME	What's that? My babe! Return'd? Oh, no!
FAIRY	Oh, yes! As I shall swiftly show.
DAME	Wait! How d'you put a nappy on? It's twenty years since she's been gone, She's sure to need a change by now, And I just can't remember how. No matter, where's my tiny mite?
FAIRY	She stands beside thee on thy right.
DAME	(looking L.) Simon? Oh, right. (Turns R.) You mean -

FAIRY	Yes, Joan.
DAME	Ooh, how my tiny mite has grown. Come to your mother's arms, my dear. (Holds out arms.)
JOAN	My mother! Did I rightly hear? (Embraces DAME.)
DAME	Such rapture I can hardly bear, Not just one daughter, but a pair.
SIMON	And that's not all you've gain'd. There's me. I am your son-in-law to be. I popp'd the question half-way down, And then fell off and hit my crown. She sent her answer down express.
JOAN	I fell off too to tell him 'yes'.
DAME	There's marriage in the air, lik 'flu. Whoever next, I wonder? (DAISY enters U.L.)
DAISY	Moo! (Whispers coyly in DAME's ear.)
DAME	O, bless her little cotton socks! She's found herself a nice young ox. Well, that must surely be the lot.
FAIRY	Tarry awhile, ye'll find 'tis not. I read the secrets of the mind, And know the King to wed's inclin'd.
DAME	He's never. Kingie, is this true?
KING	(crossing to her) It is, dear lady, and to you. You have so suddenly accru'd So large an increase in your brood, I feel a father's hand they'll need. Will you accept me?
DAME	Yes, indeed!
FAIRY	Now, really there no more can be. (Enter DEMON R.)
DEMON	There can, sweet Fairy, you and me.

	I have decided not to die,
	But at goodness to have a try,
	If you will help me learn the way.
FAIRY	Ye leave me naught but 'yes' to say.
KING	Well, isn't that delightful, then?
	We'll all be wed together.
DAME	When?
KING	As soon as poss, if not before.

(BUBBLE and SQUEAK peer on anxiously D.R.)

BUBBLE	I think it's safe.
SQUEAK	Are you quite sure?
BUBBLE	No one's fighting.

(They come onstage.)

KING	Ah, there you are.
	Go, tell my people near and far
	A gala wedding day's at hand,
	The finest ever in the land.
SQUEAK	Who's getting splic'd then?
ALL COUPLES	We are.
SQUEAK	Coo!
	Four couples?
SIMON	Yes.

(DAISY nudges SIMON.)

No, five, her too.

BUBBLE	'Twill be a bumper wedding feast.
	Our work's cut out, to say the least.
SQUEAK	Then first we'd better dust the abbey.
BUBBLE	Yes, yes, it is a little shabby.

(Exeunt BUBBLE and SQUEAK R.)

FAIRY	Now ev'ry loose end's neatly tied,
	For ev'ry bridegroom's found a bride.
	And all for joy can sing and shout
	So let the wedding bells ring out!

(Bells start chiming. <u>MUSIC 65.</u> WEDDING BELLS.)

ALL   Ring out the wedding bells
       This happy, happy day,
For joy has come to us
       And we must bid it stay.
The world is pairing off
       By two and two and two -
All that matters now is you for
       Me and me for you.
The bells are ringing
       And the sky is full of song -
'May love bring happiness
       And may your life be long'.
Voices rais'd in singing
       And the lovely music swells
To join in chorus with those
       Golden wedding bells.

(ALL go off L. except DAME and DAISY who go off R. Traverse tabs close towards end of number.)

ACT TWO

Scene Eleven - BEAUTY PARLOUR

(As soon as tabs are in DAME runs on R.)

DAME: We've gone the wrong way, Daisy. (Calling to L.) Hey, wait for us! (Calling to R.) Come on, Daisy, hurry up!

(Enter DAISY R. carrying - in her teeth or suspended round her neck - a large bag on which is written 'DAISY'S BEAUTY BAG'. The bag contains: a handkerchief, a tin of 'CHERRY BLOSSOM' and a boot brush, a large prop mascara box and large brush, a mop head for a powder puff, large prop comb and a wedding veil.)

Oh, you vain old thing. You want me to smarten you up for the wedding, do you?

(DAISY nods coyly.)

(Taking bag.) All right, then. I'll polish your nails first. What colour do you fancy? How about Cherry Blossom? (Takes out tin.) That's a nice dark shade of black.

(DAISY considers, with head on one side, then nods.)

Right.

(DAME bends over to get boot brush as DAISY raises L. hooves and knocks her down.)

Not too much enthusiasm, dear. (Rises and quickly polishes first rear and then front hoof.) Now the others.

(DAISY puts L. hooves down and bring R. ones up just as DAME bends forward to deal with them and receives them in the face.)

Oops! A nasty touch of foot and mouth. (Polishes R. hooves and moves back to bag.) Now we'll deal with the face next. How does Modom feel about a little cascara?

(DAISY is horrified.)

Sorry, dear, I meant mascara.

(DAISY nods, relieved. DAME replaces boot brush in bag and gets out mascara box and brush. She holds box in front of DAISY's mouth.)

Spit.

(DAISY spits.)

Thank you.   (Mascaras DAISY's eyelashes.) Now just a dab of powder.

(Replaces mascara brush and takes out mophead and powders DAISY so energetically that she sneezes.)

Bless you. Here.

(Replaces puff and takes out handkerchief, which she offers to DAISY to blow her nose, which she does quite genteelly, assisted by ORCHESTRA.)

That's a good girl.

(Blows own nose, rather less genteelly, also assisted by ORCHESTRA. DAISY looks shocked.)

Ooh, I think that must have been a rude word in cow language. I do beg your pardon, Daisy.

(DAISY grants it.)

Anyway, I've finished beautifying you now, dear.

(DAISY shakes head and turns round to present her hind quarters.)

What? Ah, of course, you want me to run a comb through your coiffure.   (Replaces handkerchief and takes out prop comb to comb the tuft of DAISY's tail.)   And now for the finishing touch. Turn round, Daisy. Daisy!   (Picks up DAISY's tail and uses it as a speaking tube.) Daisy, would you come and join me, please?

(DAISY turns round.)

(Replaces comb and takes out wedding veil.) Thank you. And here's your wedding veil. (Puts it on DAISY.)   That's it. Oh, you do look a treat.

(DAISY whispers anxiously in DAME's ear.)

What's that, dear?

(DAISY whispers again.)

Oh, you don't need to worry about the ring. Your intended will wear that in his nose.

(Peal of wedding bells.)

Goodness, there go those wedding bells again and I haven't started on myself yet. Come on, Daisy, you must help me now.

(DAISY nods.)

We'll have to hurry.

(Bends to pick up bag. DAISY butts her in behind to hurry her.)

Don't overdo it though, Daisy.

(DAISY starts pushing DAME off L.)

Careful, dear. Ouch! If you carry on like that you'll spoil your veil, to say nothing of my - OW! Exactly!

(As they disappear off L. tabs open for Scene Twelve. MUSIC 66.)

ACT TWO

Scene Twelve - THE BEANFEAST AT BEANSTALK HALL

(Full stage. Palace-like decor with beanstalk motif. Balustrade cut-out at back of rostrum. Steps down in C. of front of rostrum. CHORUS enter L. and R. on rostrum, come down steps two by two, bow D.C. and divide to form diagonal lines L. and R. They are followed by the PRINCIPALS, who, after they have taken their bow D.C., form diagonal lines in front of CHORUS starting: DEMON from L. on rostrum and FAIRY from R. who clear to L. and R: GIANT from L. clearing L: DAISY from L. clearing L: BUBBLE from R. and SQUEAK from L. both clearing R: KING from L. clearing L: JOAN from R. clearing R: SIMON from L. clearing R: DAME from L. clearing L: FANFARE MUSIC 67. FELICIA enters R. and JACK L. and meet in C. of rostrum. ALL turn in to them.)

ALL — Hurray!

(JACK and FELICIA move down to C., take their bow and others move into a straight line with them. CHORUS move up and form a line on rostrum.)

JACK — Good friends, our tale's no more to give.

FELICIA — We'll happy ever after live.

JOAN and SIMON — And so will we.

KING and DAME — And us as well.

FAIRY and DEMON — We hope to, too.

DEMON — But time will tell.

JACK — So ere you go upon your way,
There's but one thing we'd like to say -

ALL — Happy New Year to all of you.

DAME — And Daisy has a message -

DAISY — Moo!

MUSIC 68. WEDDING BELLS - Reprise

ALL   The bells are ringing,
                       And we wish you with our song
                That you'll find happiness
                     Throughout the New Year long.
                Voices rais'd in singing
                     And the lovely music swells
                To join in chorus with those
                     Golden wedding bells.

                CURTAIN

FURNITURE AND PROPERTY PLOT

ACT ONE
Scene One

Set:
  By Dame Durden's dairy R:
    Mop
    Maypole with coloured ribbons U.C.

Offstage L:
  Two poles (BUBBLE and SQUEAK)
  Sedan chair (KING)
  Motorised hand-drawn milk float with sign 'DURDEN'S DAIRY' and
    'DR'NKA PINTA MILKA (STOUTA) DAY' (DAME)
  Rifle and little white flag (SQUEAK)
  Cannon ball (SQUEAK)
  Large prop cannon (SQUEAK)

Offstage R:
  Blindfold (SIMON)
  Large pin (steel knitting needle) (SIMON)

Personal
  FAIRY: Wand

Scene Two

Offstage R:
  Sling, footsling, crutch (BUBBLE)
  Large head bandage and large box marked with a red cross and the
    words 'SECOND AID' (SQUEAK)
    In it:
      Bottle labelled 'Whisky'
      Pair of forceps
      Huge hypodermic syringe
      Large prop thermometer
      Camera
  Bundle of forms (KING)

Scene Three

Offstage L:
  Milking stool and pail (SIMON)
  Market stall (DAME)
    On it:
      Brace and bit
      Pot of glue
      Pot of red, pot of blue and pot of orange paint
      Painting brush
      Two sets of butter patters

    Slab of butter
    Bowl marked 'EGGS'
    A hen
    Bottle of milk
    Two little pullovers (one a Fair Isle)
    Slab of cheese
  Rope halter (JACK)

Offstage R:
  Lantern on pole (NIGHT WATCHMAN)
  Bundle of forms (BUBBLE)
  Stub of pencil (SQUEAK)
  Tray with necksling and waistband (PIEMAN)
    On it:
      Five pies (one rather green and one breakable)

Scene Four

Offstage L:
  Bag of gold (DEMON)
  Book labelled 'LETT'S DEMON'S DIARY' (DEMON)
  A rose (DEMON)
  False nose (DEMON)
  Wooden ball to be thrown on from L.
  Woollen shawl to be thrown on from L.

Offstage R:
  Shawl, cloak, false nose (FAIRY)

To descend from flies:
  Large bag labelled 'COKE' (on line)
  A cloak

Scene Five

Set:
  Chair L.C.
  Stove L.
    On shelf above stove:
      Teapot containing Guinness
      Cup, saucer and spoon
      Glass and saucepan

Offstage R:
  Diaphanous cloak (FAIRY)
  Sword (CHORUS GIRL)

ACT TWO
Scene Six

Set:
  Bag of flour fitted on wire to rise up and down on beanstalk
  Check JACK's sword

Offstage R:
  Long jagged sword shaped like lightning flash (LIGHTNING)

Off the Beanstalk U.C:
  Rope (DAME, BUBBLE, SQUEAK and SIMON)
  Small pouch haversack (DAME)
    In it:
      Two boy scout dolls
  Roll of laundry: large nightie, pair of bloomers, corsets (SIMON)

Offstage L:
  Key ring with several large keys (GIANT)
  Harp (DEMON)

Scene Eight

Set:
  Large table C. in front of rostrum
  Giant's chair behind table or chair seat built on rostrum
    R. of chair:
      Giant's club
  Large oven D.R. with practical door and two holes with covers on top
  Chains and large padlock (to chain FELICIA to rostrum at R. of table)

Offstage L:
  Very long cloak (SIMON)
  Harp (GIANT)

Offstage R:
  Check sword (JACK)
  Sheets of music, prop hen with gold egg attached (JOAN)
  Bottle of smelling salts to descend from flies

Scene Nine

Offstage L:
  Tray with neck sling and waistband (KING)
    On it:
      Baby's knitted bonnet with small crown attached
      Crown attached to schoolboy's cap
      Very large crown
      Very squashed crown

Scene Ten

Set:
   Hen and concealed gold square egg at foot of beanstalk
   Gold eggs in haversack for DAME
   Check sword (JACK)

Scene Eleven

Offstage R:
   Large bag on which is written 'DAISY'S BEAUTY BAG' (DAISY)
   In it:
      Tin of 'Cherry Blossom'
      Boot brush
      Large prop mascara box with large brush mop head for powder puff
      Large prop comb
      Wedding veil
      Handkerchief

INSTRUCTIONS FOR MAKING PROPS

Sedan Chair	Light wood frame about 5' 6" x 2' x 2', floorless but covered with painted canvas to about half its height on the sides and back. Half door opening outwards in front. Handles on each side of interior for King to hold it by. Roof made of paper perforated in a star shape.
Milk Float	Painted cut-out about 5' high x 4' long, mounted on shallow platform fitted with four pram wheels. Stick-handle fitted on front of cut-out.
Cannon	Barrel made of chicken wire covered with painted canvas and enclosing it at one end. This is held by an axle of thickish dowelling which pierces it about half-way along its length, the ends of the dowelling being fixed in two uprights of wood, about 2' high, which are mounted on a small platform no more than 2' square and running on trolley wheels. Slot in top of barrel in which is inserted a small wooden lever. This is made to pivot on the dowelling, and attached to the end of the lever inside the barrel, by a loose bolt or something which will allow it to swivel, is a piece of wood to act as a sort of piston. Thus, when the lever is pulled back the piston will be thrust forward

	to push out the cannon ball. It must, however, be carefully arranged so that it pushes the ball only just clear of the end of the barrel.
Cannon Ball	Painted canvas filled with material.
Market Stall	Light wood frame about 3' high x 3' 6" long x 1' 6" deep, covered on sides and front with painted canvas and on top with hardboard. The back can be left open. The frame is fitted with trolley wheels. A hardboard banner reading 'DAME DURDEN'S DAIRY PRODUCE' is attached by wooden supports which rise about 3' from the front of the stall.

N.B. If stacking space is limited it is a good idea to make such things as the sedan chair, the stove in Scene 5 and the oven in Scene 8 so that they can be folded flat when not in use.

MUSIC PLOT

ACT ONE

1. Overture

Scene One

2.	Opening Chorus 'MAYDAY'	Chorus
3.	Bubble and Squeak music	Orchestra
4.	King music	"
5.	Bubble and Squeak music, reprise 3	"
6.	" " " " " "	"
7.	Jack's entrance music	"
8.	Bubble and Squeak music, reprise 3	"
9.	'I WANT TO LIVE'	Jack and Chorus
10.	Fairy music	Orchestra
11.	Demon music	"
12.	Dame Durden's entrance music	"
13.	'ALSO RAN'	Dame and Chorus
14.	Princess Felicia's entrance music	Orchestra
15.	Bubble and Squeak music, reprise 3	"
16.	King music, reprise 4	"
17.	'ENJOYING MYSELF'	Felicia and Chorus
18.	Simple Simon's entrance music	Orchestra

19.	Bubble and Squeak music, reprise 3	Orchestra
20.	King music, reprise 4	"
21.	'JUMPING JOAN'	Joan
22.	'JUMPING JOAN', reprise 21	Joan and Simon
23.	Giant music, etc.	Orchestra
24.	'SO SHOULD WE'	Jack and Felicia
25.	Demon music, reprise 11	Orchestra
26.	King music, reprise 4	"
27.	Bubble and Squeak music, reprise 3	"
27a.	Bubble and Squeak music, reprise 3	"
28.	Daisy's entrance music	"
29.	Fanfare	"
30.	'MAYDAY', reprise 2 (Continue, orchestra only as link to next scene.)	Ensemble

Scene Two

31.	Demon music, reprise 11	Orchestra
32.	Bubble and Squeak music, reprise 3 very slowly	"
33.	'ETIQUETTE' (Continue, orchestra only, as link to next scene.)	King, Bubble and Squeak

Scene Three

34.	'MARKET DAY'	Ensemble
35.	'NOT OUT LOUD'	Jack and Felicia
36.	Spanish music	Orchestra
37.	'MEMORIES'	Dame
38.	Demon music, reprise 11	Orchestra
39.	Giant music, etc.	"
40.	Scene finale (Continue, orchestra only, as link to next scene.)	Jack and Chorus

Scene Four

41.	Demon music, reprise 11	Orchestra
42.	Fairy music, reprise 10	"
43.	" " " "	"
	(Continue as link to next scene.)	

Scene Five

44.	Fairy music, reprise 10	Orchestra
45.	Spell music	"
46.	Magic music	"
47.	Ballet	Fairy and Chorus

48.	Scene finale, reprise 40	Orchestra

ACT TWO

49.	Entr'acte	

Scene Six

50.	'INCANTATION'	Demon and Chorus
51.	'OUR LOVE'	Jack and Joan
52.	'YODELLING'	Dame, Simon, Bubble and Squeak
53.	Elements entrance and chase music ('Here We Go Round The Mulberry Bush')	Orchestra
54.	Giant music	Giant
55.	'GIANTS AIN'T WHAT THEY USED TO BE' (Continue, orchestra only, as link to next scene.)	Giant

Scene Seven

56.	'MOO, MOO, MOO' (Continue, orchestra only as link to next scene.)	Dame, Daisy and Audience

Scene Eight

57.	'LOST LOVE'	Felicia
58.	'ROCK-A-BY, BABY'	Ensemble
59.	Confusion and fight music	Orchestra
60.	Demon music, reprise 11	"
61.	Fairy music, reprise 1	"

Scene Nine

62.	'THE GOOD OLD DAYS'	King
63.	Running music (Continue as link to next scene.)	Orchestra

Scene Ten

64.	Demon music, etc.	Orchestra
65.	'WEDDING BELLS' (Continue, orchestra only, as link to next scene.)	Ensemble

Scene Eleven

66.	'WEDDING BELLS', reprise 65 as link to next scene and music for the walk-down.	Orchestra

Scene Twelve

67.	Fanfare	Orchestra
68.	'WEDDING BELLS', reprise 65	Tutti

www.ingramcontent.com/pod-product-compliance
Ingram Content Group UK Ltd.
Pitfield, Milton Keynes, MK11 3LW, UK
UKHW021843210426
5322IPUK00022B/434